First Comes Marriage

Modern Relationship Advice from the Ancient Wisdom of Arranged Marriages

Reva Seth

A FIRESIDE BOOK
PUBLISHED BY SIMON & SCHUSTER
New York London Toronto Sydney

Fireside
A Division of Simon & Schuster, Inc.
1230 Avenue of the Americas
New York, NY 10020

First Fireside trade paperback edition June 2008

FIRESIDE and colophon are registered trademarks of Simon & Schuster, Inc.

For information about special discounts for bulk purchases,
please contact Simon & Schuster Special Sales at 1-800-456-6798 or
business@simonandschuster.com.

The names and identifying details of some individuals in this book have
been changed.

Designed by Jan Pisciotta

Manufactured in the United States of America

10   9   8   7   6   5   4   3   2   1

Library of Congress Cataloging-in-Publication Data

Seth, Reva.
    First comes marriage : modern relationship advice from the ancient
wisdom of arranged marriages / by Reva Seth.
        p. cm.
    "A Fireside Book."
    1. Arranged marriage. I. Title.

HQ802.S48 2008
646.7'7—dc22   2007039256

ISBN-13: 978-1-4165-6172-9
ISBN-10:   1-4165-6172-2

*For my parents, Manju and Raj, my brother Ravi,
and of course Rana and darling Seth. Each of you, in your own
way, inspires me more than you'll ever know. And certainly more
than I ever have a chance to tell you. Thank you.*

Contents

Acknowledgments

This book literally wouldn't have been possible without all the women who so kindly agreed to speak with me and answer all of my questions. And then all my follow-up questions. And then a request to see if they could please pass on my name to any friends who might also talk to me. Thank you again for sharing so much of yourselves and your stories with me.

I also want to thank everyone who wrote e-mail introductions, passed on phone numbers, or suggested people whom I could talk to. This book also wouldn't have happened without the help and vision of my agent, Michelle Wolfson; Lindsey Pollak; and my editor, Michelle Howry. Thank you for making this experience so enjoyable! Please note that while all of the following stories and characters are real, both names and any identifying details have been changed to protect the privacy of those involved in this project.

Introduction

First Comes Marriage . . . Seriously?

Are you sick of random dates that seem to go nowhere? Ready to move on to the next stage in your life? Wondering why you never seem to meet your Mr. Right or find the commitment you want? Or are you in a committed relationship and worried that your boyfriend or fiancé may not be the perfect soul mate you always dreamed of?

If any of these sound like your current experience, then this book has some answers for you—answers and insight that come from arranged marriages.

When it comes to dating and relationships, the arranged-marriage approach has only one focus: fostering commitment and marriage. It's not about dating for fun or dating for the experience, or wasting months or years agonizing over the issues you need to overcome before you think you can get what you want out of both life and love.

It's not about hotties, cuties, sexual chemistry, or soul mates.

Instead, it's about finding the right partner, making the decision, and getting on with building a life of purpose and marital contentment together. That's pretty much what arranged marriages are all about. And this book is all about sharing concepts, tips, and strategies from arranged marriages in a way that all of us can use to identify an ideal mate and maintain a happy relationship, not just for now but for life.

These are life-changing lessons that will work for you, regardless of your age, culture, or past relationship experiences. And don't worry; it's not about convincing you to have an arranged marriage (I didn't!), but about understanding how you can make that approach work for you.

But wait . . .

Relationship advice from arranged marriages?

I know, I know. The idea of dating or relationship advice based on—or even in the same time zone as—the arranged-marriage experience seems completely strange. Backward. Ancient.

If that's what you're thinking, I don't blame you at all. Until quite recently, I would have completely agreed with you. But keep reading and you'll see how and why the arranged-marriage approach is both a proven route to a stable and happy relationship and particularly insightful when it comes to many of our contemporary dating and love dilemmas.

So if I didn't have an arranged marriage, how did I learn so much about this approach and how it can help us?

I learned these lessons through five years of research and more than three hundred interviews with women in arranged marriages. And along the way, I found that arranged marriages have a lot to teach us about dating, love, and long-term happiness. From finding a great partner to falling in love, sharing a home, building a family and—yes—hot sex, arranged marriages offer amazingly practical and effective relationship strategies. And the best part is that you don't actually need to *have* an arranged marriage to feel the benefits.

No matter how counterintuitive it may sound, the arranged-marriage approach to relationships offers lessons and guidelines that are increasingly relevant to the modern dating scene. But until now, these lessons have been largely ignored and overlooked, even though they are lessons that many of us can benefit from tremendously.

I firmly believe that there has never been a better time to

be a woman than right now. Think about it: compared to any other moment in history, we have unlimited freedom for opportunity, fun, and sexual adventure. And then, when we decide we're ready, we can also have a stable, fulfilling marriage and family. But there's one catch: finding and sustaining and *enjoying* marriage seems to be getting harder and harder. That's one reason why women are increasingly taking lessons from alternative models from the past (remember *The Rules,* anyone?) and, as in this book, using these models to modify their approach to commitment and lasting love.

According to Marian Salzman, coauthor of *Next Now: Trends for the Future,* "Today is the era of the arranged couple who fall in love around the birth of the first child. It sounds traditional, but in some ways so much of the future is back to the past, turbo-charged."

Increasingly, both men and women are realizing that the fantasy of randomly meeting and instantly recognizing "the one" is unlikely to happen on its own. So instead of passively waiting, they are deciding that practical, pro-active measures must be taken. Just as in an arranged marriage, these are measures that take a more direct, down-to-earth, and ultimately successful approach to long-term relationship success. "This is about picking a marriage partner—not about falling into bed for a world-class romance," says Salzman, whose trend forecasts are based on pattern recognition and the issues that style makers are talking about. "There is a newfound interest in letting someone else solve the love dilemma," she explains. "We're on option overload, and we're maxed out in terms of time, and we'd all love a partner. So it makes sense to enlist those who know us best to forge a proper and satisfying match."

Much of this is thanks to the Internet. From chat rooms to online dating services, the Web has essentially become our electronic yenta. *Time* magazine estimates that approximately 40 million Americans regularly log on to dating websites and services. Online ads, matchmakers, and speed dating are no longer considered to be the hallmark of people who are "desperate." The old stigmas that came with using these methods to find a partner are quickly disappearing, especially since the participants are often confident, busy professionals who are increasingly trying to search out partners the way they would a new job.

The statistics are compelling. For instance, a 2005 survey by the Pew Internet & American Life Project showed that 15 percent of U.S. adults knew someone who had had a serious relationship with or married a person whom he or she met online, and 31 percent knew someone who has used an online dating service.

Some websites even feel like modern versions of ancient traditions. Consider how social networking sites such as Facebook, MySpace, and LinkedIn act like social registries where you can "verify" a potential mate's social standing, appearance, and future prospects. On these sites you can even ask a mutual friend for an introduction to a complete stranger—as is the custom for arranged marriages.

A Marriage Arranged by America?

If the idea of your parents or extended family picking out your husband seems strange, then just imagine leaving it to a group of network executives or worse—the American viewing public!

In her book *The Meaning of Wife*, Anne Kingston discusses the success of Fox Network's *Who Wants to Marry a Millionaire,* or, as she describes, "The commercialized update of the Cinderella tale." This was the show where fifty women between the ages of 19 and 43 were selected from a pool of over a thousand women who sent in videotaped biographies. The lucky fifty then got to compete to become the bride of a millionaire they had never met. Oh yeah, and they also got to take home an Isuzu Trooper and a $35,000, 3-carat engagement ring! So how was the bride selected? Well, the groom, a motivational speaker cum stand-up comic cum real estate tycoon, asked the women a series of questions, ranging from what they would do if they found a woman's name and phone number in their new husband's pocket to whether they wanted to have children.

The success of this show (the final episode on February 15, 2000, drew more than 22 million viewers) led to several other spin-off shows along the same lines, including *The Bachelor*, *The Bachelorette*, *Joe Millionaire*, *Married by America*, and *Race to the Altar*.

Why am I bringing this up? My point is that arranged marriages aren't as foreign as you might think. The overwhelming response to these TV show setups seems to indicate that more and more people are interested in alternative methods for finding a life partner. Although I'm not sure how I'd feel about millions of people voting on my future happiness!

Online dating, matchmaking, and other assisted-dating services are growing in popularity (come on, admit it: you've watched *The Bachelor*—or at least *The Bachelorette*!). Why? Because, sadly, most women in our society have been groomed to think that one day our wealthy, handsome Mr. Right will just walk into our lives (with little or no effort on our part) and lead us away to blissful lives of happily ever after. We have been taught to believe in a fairy tale, and many of us spend our twenties, our thirties, and even our forties waiting for that fairy tale to come true. And when it doesn't happen, we turn to the Internet.

Could it happen? Well, theoretically it could. Will it? Probably not. But the belief or hope, however faint, that it might is what leaves so many women unhappy and alone. I want to change all that for you and for anyone you know and care about who's stuck in this situation. And I know that the answer can be found in these love lessons from arranged marriages. Here's why.

- Arranged marriages don't leave love up to chance.
- Arranged marriages don't require you to passively wait for love to find you.
- Arranged marriages are suited to each person's unique relationship and life needs.
- Arranged marriages offer women an approach that is proven to lead to stable and fulfilling relationships.

No matter what you know, or think you know, about arranged marriages, it's time to pause and give them a chance to show you what you can learn from their success—especially since the secrets I will share are proven strategies for finding and creating a fulfilling, happy, healthy relationship.

What, Exactly, Is an Arranged Marriage?

Before we go any further, let's get clear on what arranged marriages really are. Unless you grew up with or have some firsthand experience of them, I'll bet that the words "arranged marriage" don't conjure up visions of happy, committed couples or loving families.

Instead, "arranged marriage" too often conjures the unfortunate vision of very young poverty-stricken girls crying as they are forced by their families to marry older men. The HBO series *Big Love* and its creepy compound also come to mind. Tragically, this sort of thing does happen. However, that's not an arranged marriage; it's a *forced* marriage, and that's something completely different. Unlike forced marriages, arranged marriages are entirely based on the consent and full cooperation of both parties.

One of the reasons most people know very little about arranged marriage is that it's a topic that's been negatively represented (or, at best, ignored) by the media. While movies like *The Namesake* are starting to change this, it's going to be a very gradual process.

Really, probably one of the best-known mainstream examples of an ultimately happy arranged marriage is between Apu and his Indian bride, Manjula, on *The Simpsons* (bear with me here for a moment!). Despite trying to wiggle out of the arrangement, Apu is won over after meeting Manjula on their wedding day and the two are shown falling in love. Their marriage is generally portrayed as being both happy and loving—despite the birth of octuplets, his workaholic ways at the Kwik-E-Mart, and an instance of infidelity by Apu with the squishy lady (not that bad when you consider that Homer goes on a drunken bender in Vegas and ends up married to Vegas Lady).

Besides cartoon characters, do any other positive portrayals of arranged marriage come to your mind? Probably not. And the misunderstandings, stereotypes, and lack of knowledge around arranged marriages are among the reasons that the wisdom of this approach has (until now!) been largely overlooked.

Basically, an arranged marriage can be defined as a marriage organized by a third party and based on considerations other than love, intimacy, and physical or sexual attraction. In other words, arranged marriages pretty much exclude everything that we normally associate with the idea of marriage!

As with any relationship scenario, the exact details of how couples get together can vary greatly. However, the way it generally works is that once a person agrees to have an arranged marriage, his or her parents, relatives, and close family friends preselect and investigate possible candidates. They do this by consulting biographies, third-party testimonials, photos, and possibly even horoscopes. The final decision is based on a variety of criteria, including age, education, professional prospects, and family.

The idea behind arranged marriages is that although the couple is not in love when they enter the relationship, feelings of affection and intimacy will grow as they start to build their lives and their family together.

Their common expectations, as well as their shared socioeconomic, religious, political, and cultural backgrounds, contribute to this process. As Dr. Robert Epstein, editor-in-chief of *Psychology Today*, commented in a 2003 *Psychology Today* article: "Research suggests . . . that many people in arranged marriages fall in love over time. A study by Gupta and Singh, for example, shows that love in romantic marriages declines steadily over a ten-year period, but that love in arranged marriages increases over the same period, surpassing that of romantic marriages after about five years. So the experience of people in arranged marriages shows that love can be learned."

Today, many couples who decide to have an arranged marriage try to meet or speak at least once or twice before deciding whether or not to commit to the relationship. I've even heard of a trend among wealthy Indian families of discreetly allowing the arranged couple to go away for a couple of days together. This takes place after the engagement is agreed to, but before it is announced publicly. The (ever practical!) idea is that it saves on the cost of lavish engagement parties and weddings, just in case one party backs out of the arrangement for some reason.

However, many couples from previous generations—and still today—never actually see or speak with one another until after the wedding ceremony. It sounds crazy, but it works. In part, the success is due to the expectations of the couple. Arranged marriages work because both parties come into the relationship believing that they are well matched and that they can and will be happy sharing a life together in a lasting and mutually beneficial partnership.

Research published in *Psychology Today* confirms this. In the study, sixty complete strangers were paired into couples and told at the outset that they were very similar to each other. Following this briefing, all of these men and women immediately fell into comfortable and intimate exchanges with each other. Their behavior prompted the researchers to conclude that the feelings and behaviors that make up a sense of closeness emerge very early in a relationship, possibly within the first ten minutes, and that they are clearly heavily influenced by each person's initial expectations. Philosopher Alain de Boton even asserts that low expectations are one of the major predictors of happiness—the lower your expectations, the more likely your life is to exceed them!

So What Do I Know About All of This?

Okay, okay, I know. No matter how it's explained or rationalized, the idea of marrying a person who is effectively a stranger (no matter how much someone tells you you'll get along) still seems more than a little crazy, doesn't it?

I agree! And that's probably why I've been completely fascinated with arranged marriages since I was 8 years old and first realized that my parents, unlike those of my friends or the people I saw on TV, had never actually dated. In a family not ordinarily known for our speed or efficiency, my parents nonetheless managed to become engaged after two brief meetings (never alone). Two weeks later they were married and moved from India to Canada.

But beyond having parents in an arranged marriage, what actually makes me qualified to share the benefits and lessons of this life choice? I'm not trained as a psychologist, a relationship counselor, or even a journalist (I actually went to law school).

And while my parents did have an arranged marriage, I didn't grow up in an overly traditional Indian family. I started dating in high school, lived with one of my boyfriends after college, and spent a lot of my early twenties thinking about meeting "the one." Really, all fairly typical.

But I have always been incredibly interested in arranged marriages. Whether it was a cousin having one, a family friend looking for prospects, or just my brother and I teasing each other about possible matches, I couldn't get arranged marriages out of my mind. Maybe it was the dichotomy that I felt existed between my life and my mother's: the fact that in the all-white suburb of New Jersey where I grew up, I was the only one of my friends with parents who had never dated each other (and, interestingly, also never divorced). Or maybe it was just plain curiosity and an undeniable love of gossip. Whatever the impetus, I have been captivated by arranged marriages for years.

And by captivated, I mean I have wondered about everything from the logistics . . .

> If you've only met a few times, what's the sex like? And does it ever get better? If you don't meet until after the wedding, how do you start the conversation? And then where to from there?

. . . to the bigger questions.

> Are these couples actually happy or are they secretly pining for someone else? And if they are happy, what does that say about the whole idea of falling in love and getting married?

(If you're wondering about the same things, I promise that this book will satisfy your curiosity about these and many other aspects of arranged marriages.)

At the family events I attended growing up, I would (and to

be honest, still do) try to observe the differences between the arranged-marriage group and the love matches. I was hoping to see a blatant distinction between the two and felt that the love couples should somehow radiate a sort of blissful glow of compatibility or exhibit some incredible chemistry. But of course they never did. Which I found even more fascinating and which led me to question my beliefs about love, relationships, and life-long compatibility.

So, in 2000, I decided to start interviewing women in arranged marriages to learn more about them. My initial idea was, very generally, to start collecting their stories, both out of interest and in the hope of finding answers to the sorts of questions I had always wondered about (but would never actually ask my own mother).

Despite having grown up around arranged marriages that seemed happy—including that of my parents who, after over thirty-three years of marriage, always seem to have something to laugh and talk about—I hadn't actually expected that the overwhelming majority of women I spoke with would seem so genuinely satisfied, happy, and confident about their marriages. To be honest, it was a complete shock.

An even greater surprise was the way in which their suggestions and advice seemed so applicable to the relationship issues and problems that I and the other women I knew at the time were facing as single, urban women drifting from date to date, not really sure where we were going or what we were looking for.

To be honest, it took me a while to accept and acknowledge this—since the idea that *they* (women in arranged marriages) would end up teaching *me* (a modern, liberated woman) anything about dating, relationships or marriage was just about the last thing I expected from these interviews! But that's exactly what happened. And the results of my interviews were so unexpected and paradigm-shifting that I felt I had to share them.

The Interviews

My lifelong curiosity on this topic led me to speak with over three hundred women who all had chosen to have an arranged marriage. The women spanned the economic range. The youngest was just barely in her early twenties and the oldest was in her late eighties. The interviewees ranged from women who worked in bakeries, to Indian royalty, to New York bankers and suburban moms.

Some, particularly the younger ones, had dated and had relationships before deciding on an arranged marriage. A few had been divorced or widowed, while others had had little or no relationship or sexual experience before marriage. I met my interviewees through ads I placed online, in newspapers, in community centers, and in ethnic grocery stores in the United States, the United Kingdom, and Canada. They were members of my family, the mothers of friends, friends of friends, their family friends—essentially, anyone and everyone who was willing to talk to me about this topic and share their personal stories and experiences. I met with some in person over the course of a few days or weeks; with others we spoke over the phone or through e-mail. Since I was doing these interviews out of personal interest, I let the conversations evolve organically, with no set times or mandatory questions.

Although we don't hear much about it, arranged marriages are actually still the norm in India, Pakistan, large parts of mainland China, and throughout Africa and the Middle East. Because of my own Indian heritage, I had the easiest access to women of this background, and about 85 percent of my interviewees were women of Indian descent. When I expanded my goal from general learning to writing a book, I reached out to a more diverse group of women in arranged marriages, including women of

Chinese, Moroccan Jewish, and Egyptian backgrounds. Stories from each of these groups appear throughout this book and inform my theories and advice.

What I Learned

As I've said, when I began speaking to women in arranged marriages, it was purely out of curiosity. I never intended my interviews to be a scientific or sociological study—which they aren't! The idea for this book came about because of the themes I began to hear over and over again in the conversations I was having. For instance, the overwhelming majority of women in arranged marriages seemed to describe themselves as being happy and fulfilled in their marriages and genuinely pleased with the marital choice made for them. Not only was this *not* what I'd been expecting, but it was in complete contrast to the general relationship angst and culture of divorce that surrounds us in the United States.

In 2005, *USA Today* ran a greatly hyped article that the overall divorce rate in the United States is down from its previous rate of 50 percent. However, experts are saying that the decline is simply the result of the rise in couples choosing cohabitation over marriage.

In contrast, arranged marriages have an incredibly low divorce rate (estimated at approximately 5 to 7 percent), but even more than that, longitudinal studies (for example, a 2005 study by Jane Myers et al. in the *Journal of Counseling and Development*) actually show that over time, parties in arranged marriages report being both happier and more satisfied in their marriages.

I should acknowledge here that divorce is particularly frowned upon in South Asian cultures. This means that lack of divorce is not necessarily an indicator of happiness or satisfaction. However, my interviews included only a few instances of unhappy marriages. Admittedly, this group may have been self-selecting, but I believe that a similar group of three hundred love-match relationships would most likely result in fewer positive reports. It is certainly a point open to debate. While I may not be able to provide or extract statistically significant insight from my interviews, the anecdotes, observations, and advice I collected and share in this book provide plenty of evidence of this happiness.

The women I interviewed also were generous in sharing their strategies and advice that the rest of us can apply. Their advice certainly worked for me. When I began my interviews, I had just come out of a failed and much-dragged-out five-year relationship, after which I had spent most of my time and energy actively dating an ever-increasing array of Mr. Wrongs and Mr. Just-For-Nows. But the novelty of dating was definitely wearing off and I was ready to move on.

Over time, I noticed that my interviews started to change both my approach and perspective toward how and whom I was dating. And after I began applying the lessons you'll find in Secrets 1 and 2, I started to see results quickly—meeting the man who is now my husband and becoming engaged to him . . . on the seventh time we met in person! No, it wasn't love (or lust) at first sight. It was actually the result of both of us having figured out what we were looking for in a partner, being at the same life stage, recognizing that the other person had the potential to have the qualities we wanted and then, as my husband describes it, "exchanging over a hundred thousand words on e-mail" to confirm it. By the time we next met (he was in London and I was in Toronto), we both knew it was the right thing to do—despite how it looked to our friends and family! We were married less than five months later and, now, we have been happily married for just over four years and have one adorable son.

Using This Book:
The Arranged-Marriage Approach to Dating

Lesson number one: Skillful and strategic dating and a great relationship are *learned behaviors*.

In the 2003 *Psychology Today* article, "The Life of Love," Diane Sollee, the founder and director of Smart Marriages, an organization with the mandate to "help make love last," says, "Everyone wants their relationship to work. It's a goal that every single person has." As a 2005 *Time* magazine poll found, this goal is probably due to the fact that relationships and family connections are the primary source of our happiness.

It's a view that our society actively encourages—particularly the idea that we should aspire to building a family with another person. Despite this focus, we are provided very little in terms of practical advice or models of how to do it. Put it this way: so many of us spend years and thousands of dollars learning the skills to pursue the career or business we want, but we somehow still expect that our relationships should magically "just happen."

And when it comes to love, we rarely think ahead. As a general rule, we are not trained to think about how our feelings will change or evolve thirty—or even three—years into the future. We are not taught to consider what we might expect and want from our partners and relationships after the initial flush of infatuation wears away, or as we age or have children. This is one of the reasons that arranged marriages are such a valuable model: they have evolved specifically with these questions and concerns in mind.

As you read through the stories and suggestions in this book, you'll see each secret is adapted from the arranged-marriage model to apply to modern, nonarranged relationships. **I promise you that this book is most definitely *not* an attempt to convince you that arranged marriages are the better way to go!** Don't worry—I'm not suggesting that you enlist an old aunt or nosy friend of your mom's to find you a guy to marry next month. That would be a bit much! No matter how successful arranged marriages are as a model, I believe that having an arranged marriage is a culturally specific decision. And although I grew up around arranged marriages, I myself didn't actually choose to have one. But I have absolutely chosen to live by their success secrets.

The terminology I'll use to describe the application of arranged-marriage strategies to modern, nonarranged relationships is "the arranged-marriage approach." This term involves seeking and entering into relationships and marriage with a different perspective from the traditional vision of just happening to meet and fall in love with "the one" and living happily ever after with a white picket fence and 2.3 kids.

As you will see throughout the coming chapters, taking an arranged-marriage approach to relationships involves rethinking your current attitudes and expectations about love. It asks you to question whether the beliefs that you have are helping or hurting your ability to find and meet a life partner and secure a satisfying relationship. You will also find some exercises to help you apply these tips to your own life and practice the strategies presented.

This book will provide you with the lessons and principles that I've learned from my interviews with women in arranged marriages. The concepts are adapted in a way that fits with most women's modern lives, incorporating key lessons from arranged marriages into a realistic approach that any woman—single, dating, or married—can apply. These secrets will empower you to have more relationship choices, to make better choices when you are in a committed relationship, and to find greater happiness and fulfillment for the rest of your life.

See? You really can live happily ever after. Read on to learn how.

Chapter One

Your Man Doesn't Have to Be Your Best Friend

Escaping the Myth of "the One"

Tina is a 38-year-old, L.A.-based talent agent and self-professed serial dater. With short dark hair, a deep throaty laugh, and a funky vintage style, Tina gives the impression that she's a woman confident about what she wants—and pretty much used to getting it.

Except, that is, when it comes to her relationships.

"I'll be honest: I've wanted a family since, like, oh, forever!" she admits. Tina is from a large, close family and she wants at least three kids. "Obviously, I'm just waiting to find the right man," she says. "Someone who'll be a good father, a best friend for me, my intellectual and professional equal, someone who'll be exciting, share my love of literature, give me a good lifestyle, get on with my sisters, and, of course, create a hot sex life!" And she adds as an afterthought, "And he'll be someone who gives me a sense of inner peace and calm."

Does it strike you that Tina is asking for a lot? Could any real human being ever measure up?

You can—and I have—pointed this out to her, but she is unrepentant and completely unwavering in her belief that this guy is out there waiting for her. "I feel that since I have the sort of choices that my mother never did, and since I've waited all this time and walked away from guys that were close but not quite there, I think I deserve not to settle for anything less than everything I really want. Besides, if he's the right one for me, then he'll be all these things to me anyway. And there'll be nothing to worry about."

As a result, Tina has dated everyone from a stockbroker in his fifties just coming out of a divorce, to a young graduate student, to a movie stuntman who jumps off buildings and runs through fire for a living. It's all wonderfully fun and she's had some great experiences with these guys, but her dating choices are clearly not getting her what she wants—a husband.

Not only are Tina's expectations from her ideal husband incredibly high; she has another problem as well. "I feel like after the second date, I know whether he's going to be able to measure up," she tells me. So any guy who can't show that he matches all of Tina's many criteria by date number two loses his chances with her.

It's an incredibly naïve approach to love and relationships, but then, Tina suffers from a particularly modern love dilemma: she wants a man customized to her every desire and she wants him to arrive preassembled, with no work or time required on her part. Sounds a bit like a Stepford husband, doesn't it?

It may seem as if I'm criticizing Tina's desires, but I'm not. Tina's situation is so common among women today, particularly those of us in our late twenties and thirties. After all, we've dated for a long time and we're used to asking for so much from ourselves that we just don't want to settle for anything less than the perfect husband we feel we deserve.

Which brings us to the important questions that you need to

ask yourself if you want to find a life partner: What do you think a husband today is for, and why do you want one? It may sound silly, but really, your answer to this question is critical to determining your dating and relationship success.

In the past—well, really just a generation ago—the answer to this question was relatively straightforward. You needed and wanted a husband for:

- Financial support
- Kids

A husband back then was simply a necessary part of the life equation. Everyone's roles and expectations were clear: the husband was the breadwinner in the public sphere and the wife was the caretaker in the private sphere. Nothing new here, right? Well, today we don't actually *need* husbands to play any of these traditional roles, although many of us might still want them to (which, of course, is perfectly okay, too).

So where does this leave us? What's the point today of a boyfriend or husband? Or, as Maureen Dowd asked, in her eponymous book, are men necessary?

To me (and, I'm guessing, to you as well if you're reading this book), the answer is clearly yes! Don't get me wrong; doing away with the old utilitarian model of the cash-producing father and homemaking mother is definitely progress. The problem is that we've gone almost too far and instead replaced it with an even more onerous obligation of trying to find Mr. Perfect. It seems that since we no longer need husbands to bring home the bacon, we all want and feel entitled to nothing less than a soul mate. Unfortunately, we generally lack either a precise definition or a model of what that really means. The result is that, like Tina, we are somehow convinced that we'll just be able to recognize our soul mate when he comes along. No wonder so many women feel frustrated or unhappy with their relationships or the men they're meeting!

It may seem silly at first, but pause for a moment right now. Take out a pen and piece of paper. Answer these questions and be completely honest:

- What are you really hoping for from a long-term partner or husband?
- What roles do you want him to play?

To help make it easier, describe an average day in your life with this man:

- How does he interact with you first thing in the morning?
- How many times a day do you talk on the phone, e-mail, IM, or text-message each other?
- What do you talk about and how does he respond?
- How does he show his affection?
- How does he respond when you tell him about something that's bothering you?
- What do you do together after work?
- What do you do on weekends?
- What qualities or personality traits does he have?
- What activities does he share with you?
- How often do you socialize separately and together? Alone and with other people?

Chances are your fantasy contains a lot—maybe more than you ever realized. Probably more than you expect from your best friend. Probably more than any one person can deliver. That's exactly Shannon's problem.

"I Want It All!"

Shannon is 34 years old and an editor at an interior decorating magazine. She's also in the midst of launching her own home fabrics line. Although both of these ventures are fairly time-consuming, Shannon has nevertheless created a complicated dating arrangement that is definitely worthy of *Big Love.* Shannon is currently living with her boyfriend, Brent, in a tall, narrow house in Astoria, Queens, but she is also dating two other men "exclusively."

"I've been seeing Jay, a twenty-seven-year-old Ph.D. student in literature, for the past year, and Tom, a furniture designer, for a few months." All three men are aware of the arrangement and fine with it. According to Shannon, she has never been in a more fulfilling situation. "In the past, I was never really completely happy with any of my relationships; I always felt like there was something missing, that would leave me feeling frustrated or like I was settling. I love Brent, but after a year I started to feel like aspects of my personality were being neglected. I didn't want to end it, but I also didn't want to be in a situation where Brent was falling short of what I needed and I was resenting him for it." The result is that on certain nights Shannon is out with either Jay or Tom, depending on their schedules.

They established that they can come back to the house only if she clears it with Brent. Despite my disbelief, Shannon assures me that all the guys are comfortable with the arrangement. "I always tell my girlfriends that I've found the way to find the perfect man: you combine three of them! Each of them brings out a different side of me." Despite her enthusiasm for her alternative arrangement, Shannon admits that she is not sure what the future will bring. "Tom is thirty-nine and keen to start a family soon, and I don't think he sees an arrangement like this as part of his plan."

At this point, and for the first time in our conversation, her relentless optimism dips. "I mean, I know it's something that I'm going to have to face as well. This isn't exactly an arrangement I want to bring kids into. And right now, it's also something that I'm hiding from my family. I don't know . . . hopefully, the next guy I meet will be the one who really is a combo of all three of them, my real Perfect Man."

To be honest, at first I was pretty shocked by Shannon's "solution" to finding the perfect relationship—and I still don't understand how she got them all to agree to it! But then I gave it some more thought. Although most of us probably feel that we have little in common with Shannon, many women have the same unrealistic expectation that one person can satisfy our every need and desire. If a man doesn't meet *all* the requirements on our relationship laundry list, we feel that there's a problem—that we are being denied something we are entitled to. It makes sense, then, that even three men combined can't meet all of our expectations.

What makes it worse is that most of us never realize the full extent of our own relationship expectations. Instead, we just keep wondering why no one we meet seems "just right," complain that there are "no good ones out there," or question why we feel disappointed and frustrated by the men we meet or the relationships we have.

If you stopped to make a list of everything you consciously and unconsciously expect from a boyfriend or future husband, chances are that the list would look something like this.

Love	Honesty
Acceptance	Open communication
Romance	Commitment
Great sex	Doing things together
Companionship	A nice family

Friendship	Listening
Understanding	Sharing
Emotional support	A connection
Genuine intimacy	Shared personal growth
Financial support	Social
Sense of humor	Being a good father

Pretty standard? Probably for today it is. But it's unlikely that either our mothers or our grandmothers would have been looking for so much from one person. They would have been especially skeptical of ambiguous traits like having "a connection." Today, women's expectations from our lives are higher than ever. We want all the goodies that a loving, intimate relationship seems to offer, wrapped up in great packaging and on all our own terms and time lines. And while high expectations are a good thing, unrealistic expectations just set us up to feel frustrated and angry with our dates and our lives because nothing ever seems good enough.

What is it exactly that is making us both consciously and unconsciously expect so much from our men? Well, partly it's the result of all the cultural myths around what or who a husband should be. These are partly the product of the Barbie doll and Disney princess stories sold to us from childhood. And of course Hollywood, television, and magazines aren't helping. Instead, they bombard us with messages about what "real love" should be: If it's true love and he is the right one, then he should, in the words of Jerry Maguire, "complete us."

Essentially, I think all of this feeds into an ultimate female myth of rescue, in which our prince comes into our life and sweeps us off our feet, happily solving any outstanding problems, issues, or angst we may have. And along the way, he takes us into a marvelously easy future of incredible and intuitive intimacy, where he provides us with our personal version of a life of fun, fulfillment, and romance.

Because women no longer need men for survival (or even children!), there is now incredible pressure for our intimate relationships to be the primary source of strength, support, and companionship in our lives. With the decline of the extended family, a rise in dispersed communities, and the fact that we are all working longer and harder, too often our other relationships and networks fall to the side. This puts our partners under even more pressure to be the ones to fulfill all our emotional and companionship requirements—expectations that no one person (or apparently even three!) could ever actually fulfill.

When 35-year-old Paula moved to Philadelphia to join her boyfriend, Marc, it put an incredible strain on their relationship. She started looking to Marc to take the place of her old colleagues and friends and her two sisters. "I was used to having a really busy social schedule, and suddenly I was stuck alone in our rented place basically all day. When I'd complain, Marc would tell me to just call my friends and talk, but I wanted someone to meet me for coffee or an afternoon of shopping. As a result, I would insist that Marc do it with me, which neither of us really wanted."

The assumption that two people are going to fulfill each other's every need can only be a setup for relationship disappointment and, ultimately, failure. Nevertheless, we continue to believe that if we are not following this magical path, something must be wrong—with him, with us, or with the relationship.

Exercise: Breaking Up with Your Fantasy Man

If breaking up is hard to do, then breaking up with the fantasy man in your head is even harder. After all, this guy has never done anything wrong—well, apart from never showing up, that is. But since the goal is to either meet or find happiness with a real man, it's time to let go of Prince Charming.

Go all out: make a real ritual of letting go of him so you can enjoy someone real. Here are the steps to follow.

- Take the list you made earlier with all the qualities you listed and expand on them. Write down any secret scenarios that you always pictured with him and all of your over-the-top husband fantasies. (We're talking *everything* here, whether it's private planes or famous names, anything and everything that you've always secretly hoped he might be, do, or say.)

- Read over your list, take a deep breath—and shred it. Bye -bye, Prince Charming. Good riddance, I say!

Just like any real breakup, you're now entitled to an evening of gobbling down peanut butter cups and ice cream while lounging in bed in your favorite ratty pajamas.

The Grass Isn't Always Greener

Thirty-eight-year-old Jane is a nonprofit executive who married a technology sales rep named Andy while in her early twenties. At 31, she met another man at a fund-raising event whom she felt instantly attracted to, and who seemed able to give her "more in every way" than Andy. And so, after an agonizing three-year affair, she left her husband for the other man. A year and a half into the new relationship, they broke up.

Looking back, Jane now thinks that she made a mistake, and that her relationship with her husband was actually both solid and workable. But she admits that she didn't see that all those years ago when she left him. "There was always someone better around the corner, someone I thought would challenge or excite me more. What I was looking for wasn't fair to either him or me."

And that's part of the problem with our entire view of what husbands are for and what they are supposed to give us: we ignore the basics because we are always expecting and looking for *more*. According to Dr. Scott Haltzman, author of *The Secrets of Happily Married Men,* "If you hold to an ideal that may never be met, you lose the opportunity to appreciate the good qualities of what's already in front of you."

The trap that so many of us fall into is that, initially, it can seem like a new person is the answer, until they too let us down and we are left wanting again. It's a cycle that can continue indefinitely, although in Jane's case, she realized after the second time around that no one could give her what she was looking for. A new person was just offering the hope of perfection.

Toward the end of my interviews I would ask what advice each woman had for women like me about the way in which we approach men, dating, and marriage. Women most frequently pointed to the overemphasis placed on whether a partner was making us happy enough or how someone else could do it better.

"I really worry that my daughter will never be satisfied," confessed Rita, a sweet-faced 51-year-old woman who runs a small fabric boutique in New Hampshire. Her 33-year-old daughter Sari is single, living in New Jersey, and claims that all she wants is to meet someone "who would just make me really happy."

But, as Rita describes it, "She's never happy for long. Her last boyfriend was so good to her, but they only lasted seven months before she decided that he didn't pay enough attention to her. Sure enough, soon she was looking for the next one. She doesn't listen to me, but I tell her that no one will be able to really give her what she's looking for."

Psychologist Dennis Sugrue, an associate professor of clinical psychiatry at the University of Michigan Medical School and coauthor of *Sex Matters for Women,* says, "If you are looking to a partner to make you feel worthwhile, to make you feel happy, to rescue you from a boring or unhappy life, if you are seeking someone to make you feel complete or whole, well, then, you have some work to do because there are needs that are never going to be met by anyone other than yourself." Putting these demands on someone else, he says, is setting you and the relationship up for failure.

Rita's daughter Sari sounded so familiar to me. Maybe you relate to her as well. It's the situation where you meet someone and it seems like it could be good, but you keep wondering if there could be something better out there—someone who understands you more, or is more exciting, or enjoys more of what you like to do. It can become difficult to know when to accept that you've found what you want or were looking for. But if you keep looking and looking, you never stop long enough to see if the person in front of you could be a great mate.

Natalie, a 32-year-old photographer, suffers from this "grass is always greener" syndrome. None of her relationships seems to go beyond the three-month mark. "One of my college professors used to always say: 'You don't know what you don't know,' " Natalie says. "I can't remember the context that he used it in, but I'm quite sure it wasn't meant for what I interpreted as—my dating life!"

She explains, "Every time I start to relax a bit into a relationship and think, 'Okay, maybe this is what I need to make me happy,' I start having doubts along the lines of what else is out there that might be better. I wonder if this guy will satisfy my future needs, even if I don't know what those are yet."

The obvious problem here is that none of us can predict the future. Life happens, situations and people change, and along the way feelings ebb and flow. So how can you decide if a particular man will be the best life partner? Basically, you make an educated guess based on the information available. As unromantic as that may sound, it's true. And it works. Arranged marriages show that a man's values, family, and life goals are excellent predictors of what a future with that man will look like. And women in arranged marriages understand that 50 percent of the relationship's happiness and success is up to you.

Husbands: Life Partners, Not Life Savers

Arranged marriages are based on the belief that a strong marriage can be created by bringing together two similar and complementary people who have common goals and aspirations, as well as a shared approach to making the relationship work over the long term. It (always!) bears repeating that half of that long-term success is up to you.

Since women in arranged marriages don't expect to be marrying their soul mates, they enter into the relationships with far more manageable and realistic expectations about both their husbands and the relationship. They view their husbands not as their primary source of happiness or as a means of rescue, but instead, as life partners, friends, and men who will provide them with support, companionship, children, and a family life.

Fifty-four-year-old Taja met 57-year-old Ravi, her husband of almost twenty-eight years, over tea one afternoon in her parents' living room in India. Despite the formal setting and presence of family, she remembers that the conversation flowed easily. Like her, Ravi had also gone to graduate school in the United States so the two talked about their college experience, jobs, and travel hopes. As Taja describes it, "Because I wasn't in love with Ravi when I got married and he wasn't one of the suave James Bond types that I had always read and fantasized about, it meant that I didn't put him on a pedestal. I didn't expect him to be my soul mate, my best friend, and everything else all at the same time. Instead I expected that he would be a caring spouse, an interesting person, a good father and someone I would build my life with. And he has been."

And You Thought Your First Dates Were Hard . . .

Shared values and common backgrounds probably make for a strong long-term relationship, but if you've never met until after the wedding ceremony, what do you start talking about for the first time?

- "Food! We both admitted that we hadn't been able to eat anything all day (and in my case for the two days before) and we were both starving. So our first conversation was about how to order up some of the wedding leftovers."

  —Adita, 39

- "Soccer. There had been a big match that day and he wanted to know if I knew what had happened and if I followed the game."

  —Blossom, 41

- "I was so nervous that I just started to cry! He was wonderful, though. He just sat there, held my hand, and listened."

  —Kirti, 53

- "He asked what I'd thought of the day and we just talked about the wedding and our guests."

  —Sevika, 29

> • "Each other. He asked me if he was what I'd been expect-
> ing. I told him how I'd saved the picture that his family
> had sent me, and he said that he'd done the same."
>
> —Priya, 60

Since they aren't in love with their spouses when they marry, women in arranged marriages, even those who had grown up in the United States surrounded by the same cultural pressures as the rest of us, were free from all the loaded associations around what their husband should be and do with and for them. They were essentially free from all the unspoken expectations that come with the belief (or hope!) that this man would be their Mr. Right. This meant that if their husbands didn't intuit their needs, understand any personal feelings, fill their emptiness, or want to join them in their activities, then so what? They didn't interpret any of this to mean that their relationship or partner was flawed or "wrong," or that it meant they were settling and therefore wonder if someone else could do what this person couldn't or wouldn't. Realistic expectations meant that they as well as their husbands and relationships were saved from this burden.

• The result is that women in arranged marriages have a much better sense of owning their own happiness—which may seem surprising, since many people think of women in arranged marriages as giving up ownership of their destinies. However, what I found was that they seem to have no problem with assuming responsibility for meeting their own needs from a variety of different sources, including friends, family, or themselves. This approach made them much happier and allowed them to move on to meeting these needs without resenting their partners in the process (as often happens when you feel let down by your boyfriend or partner). Their attitude relieves both partners, and the relationship generally, from the incredible pressure that most other couples have.

These women accepted that their partners are not their "everything," and had instead found easy, workable solutions that made them both happy. For example, 45-year-old Anusha, whose husband hated the theater, joined a local group so she would have company when she went to the shows. Aleena, a 59-year-old receptionist in Miami, told me that one of the secrets to her happy thirty-two-year marriage is letting her husband have time to himself when he comes home while she calls her sisters and tells them about her day instead of trying to immediately engage him in conversation.

The seemingly effortless ability of women in arranged marriage to happily have a range of needs met by people other than their husbands was actually one of the first things that got me thinking that there might be lessons to learn from arranged marriages. It was probably about a year and a half into my interviews, when I was having dinner with two friends in Toronto. I was listening to one of them complain about how upset she was that her boyfriend never wanted to join her on her Saturday mornings jogs, no matter how much she asked him, and how it was starting to become a big issue between them since they were starting each weekend with a fight. Whereas before my research I probably would have instantly sympathized, I now found myself thinking, "I don't see what the big deal is! Just ask someone else."

While most people have the impression that arranged marriages are the epitome of old-fashioned, many of their practices and tenets are thoroughly modern. The women I met in arranged marriages take control of their own happiness and don't rely on a man to be the be-all and end-all of their lives. Why aren't women in nonarranged marriages more independent? Why do we want men to be everything to us? I think it's time we had a serious expectation makeover!

They may not be in love or know each other when they marry, but women entering into arranged marriages have realistic expectations. There is no ambiguity in terms of what is expected from either the husbands or the wives and no sense of unspoken or unacknowledged expectations.

In addition to the expectations being clear, they are also manageable and reachable. This means that there is no unrealistic pressure placed on the relationship, but instead the fulfillment and satisfaction that comes from being able to meet another person's essential needs and find happiness together. Each person also has a sense of developing outside and separate interests and support networks—all of which takes the focus and burden away from their partners' having to be the primary source of both company and companionship. After all, some dependency is good, but complete dependency on a partner for all one's needs is just an invitation for both partners to end up unhappy.

The correlation between expectations and happiness has been well documented. When we expect too much, it's inevitable that we will feel let down by the reality. For instance, a study published by professors James McNutly of Ohio State University and Benjamin Karnety of the University of Florida found that the people with the highest expectations for wedded bliss set themselves up for the steepest decline in happiness after the wedding.

Experts also say that it's important for couples to maintain a life beyond their partner. It's not healthy to invest all of your time and energy in your spouse. Imogen Lloyd Webber, author of *The Single Girl's Survival Guide,* cautions, "It is essential to nurture your friends, to meet with them separately since the reason the person you are with was attracted to you in the first place was that you had such a life in place. If you completely give up any independence, you will become so needy that you will be less attractive and then in danger of losing [them]."

As Pooja, a woman married for fifteen years, assured me, "I don't understand this Western idea of always being or doing things together. How does that keep things interesting?" She herself plays bridge with her friends at least twice a week without her husband (who hates cards), and has no problem going to see the art films she loves without him.

It's true that bringing outside interests into a relationship can only enrich it. The problem is that from magazines to television to banner ads on our favorite websites, we are bombarded by images of couples that are always together and blissfully focused on each other. Unlike women in arranged marriages, the implicit message is that the easiest and most likely way to experience unmitigated joy and excitement in our lives involves finding the right partner who will give us that feeling—every day, all day. Many women consider it a badge of honor to say, "My husband is my best friend." Single women often feel jealous when they hear such comments. Well, I invite you to question that feeling. Why should your husband be your best friend? Why can't you have a best friend *and* a husband? I mean, what did you do before you had this relationship? This way of living is more fun for you and it takes the pressure off the man to play both roles in your life.

Often, the excitement of a new person and the start of a relationship does make us want to spend every waking minute with the other person. There is the hope that this could be it—this could be the man who will provide us with everything that has felt lacking or missing in our lives. There's nothing wrong with these romantic feelings. But all too often these initial feelings subside, only to be replaced with a familiar sense of disappointment and frustration. As a result, we move from relationship to relationship, partner to partner, looking to find those feelings again and not realizing or acknowledging that only we can satisfy those emotional needs in ourselves.

My advice from my arranged-marriage research? Do your best not to get carried away. Your partner obviously will (and should be) a key source of day-to-day happiness. But as we've seen, he or she won't (and shouldn't be expected to) provide you with happiness (that's your job). Nor can he be held responsible for solving any life issues that might be depressing or frustrating you. (Yep, that means your career and money issues too!)

This is the challenge that 33-year-old Catharine is facing. Catharine recently moved to an apartment just outside of Seattle that's much closer to the suburb where she grew up than she likes to think about. Currently working as a junior tax associate in a small law firm, Catharine admits, "I'm pretty bored with my life. Most of the time I feel like I just don't know where I'm going or what I want."

She talks about possibly changing careers since she isn't actually interested in tax law. The only problem is that she's not sure what else to do. It's the same with moving. She's sick of Seattle and can't believe she ended up back here, hanging out with the same people she grew up with. But she really isn't drawn to any other city and doesn't know where else to go.

Filled with a sense of boredom and frustration, she's convinced that meeting the right guy and falling in love will solve all of her problems. "I'd love to meet someone that would want to move with me out of city, give me a financial cushion so I wouldn't have to work, and could help me figure out what I really want to do." In addition to solving her practical problems, Catharine thinks that he (whoever and wherever he is) will be able to "take away the depression I've felt for the past few years and bring back some excitement about the future."

Catharine's story is a common one that comes in many different forms. For instance, a close friend of mine, Alice, recently dated a man she admired because he always seemed so focused about his career. At that time, Alice was trying to decide whether she should leave her current job and go back to law school, try journalism, or get certified as a yoga teacher. "I was attracted to Peter," she recalls, "because I kept hoping on some level that his confidence in what he was doing careerwise would help me. I'm not sure if I wanted him to just tell me what to do or if I wanted someone who seemed together to give me his approval." It was when Peter broke up with her that Alice was actually able to appreciate what she had been looking to him to provide and realized that, when it came to her life and career, only she had the answers regarding what would actually make her happy. (Turns out it was a mix—journalism with some yoga thrown in.)

Catharine's and Alice's stories are certainly not unique. Nor are they particularly modern. Ultimately, all of the stories in this chapter about finding a soul mate, a hero, a savior—the one—are various versions of the age-old female myth of rescue. Too many women still believe that a prince will ride into their lives on a white horse and solve their financial problems, weight issues, career frustrations, and feelings of loneliness. But the reality is otherwise, as financial guru Barbara Stanny stated clearly in her 1999 book, *Prince Charming Isn't Coming.*

Exercise: The List

You don't have to be dating anyone right now to do this one. For this exercise, make a list of all the activities that you would like your partner (current or future) to do with you. Include absolutely everything that you've ever secretly wished your husband or boyfriend would do with you, whether it's watching your favorite sitcom, working out together, or just happily keeping you company while you do the week's grocery shopping. (Good luck with that one by the way!)

Once you've made your list, write down next to each activity all the *other* people (including just yourself) who could instead join you for that activity. Now honestly, would it really be that bad to, say, do a few of these with someone else?

The point of this exercise is to start thinking about how to start naturally looking to people other than your partner to fulfill some of your relationship requests.

Freeing yourself from the myth of "the one"—that be-all and end-all guy who solves all your problems and fulfills your every need—has numerous life-changing benefits. When you realize that a husband will enrich your life, but will not be the center of it, you will:

- **Increase your freedom.** This removes you from the passive position of believing that your happiness depends on the actions of someone else and instead enables you to take charge of your own needs.
- **Decrease dating tension.** Changing your expectations from the belief that your future husband should fulfill an incredible number of roles and needs takes you out of the common cycle of disappointment, frustration, and anger related to finding a lifelong mate.
- **Increase your chances of meeting someone with whom you can build a long-term relationship.** When what you're looking for becomes realistic, it automatically expands your pool of potentially eligible men.

Once we understand the arranged-marriage model and apply it to your life, we can see that our cultural ideal of making our husbands or boyfriends the people responsible for meeting all our needs and wants does us a great disservice. It's a fairy tale that won't *ever* be played out, since no one person can or even should have to be so much to someone else.

When it comes to dating or relationships, all these incredibly unrealistic expectations often cause us to overlook men (including the ones around us) with the potential to make us fulfilled and happy. Letting go of the ideas and expectations around what a husband or partner *should* be also frees us to let go of being angry, disappointed, or bitter throughout our dating life and ultimately our marriage relationship. And that leads to a truly happy ending.

Living This Lesson

- **Be realistic about the role of a life partner.** Women in arranged marriages view their husbands not as their primary source of happiness or as a means of rescue, but instead, as life partners, friends, and people who will provide them with support, companionship, children, and a family life.
- **Break up with the fantasy man in your head.** No man is perfect or perfectly suited to your every desire and need. Your real goal should be finding happiness and fulfillment with a real person.
- **Ditch the fairy tale.** Next time you're relaxing with a romantic comedy, take a second look and consider what the movie is really saying and promoting. Is it realistic? I doubt it.
- **Own your own happiness.** You are responsible for having your needs met from a variety of different sources, including friends, family, and yourself. Pretty empowering, don't you think?

Chapter Two

Secret #2

The Musts Are All That Matter

Your Type Might Not Be What You Think It Is

Last year was a big one for Nicole. It was her thirty-fifth birthday and the year her younger sister and two best friends both got married. It could have been the kind of situation that really depresses some people, but Nicole is more the sort of girl who focuses on all the fun of the parties, the celebrations, the excuse for wearing another little black dress. . . .

Still, she admits that since these events she finds herself thinking and telling friends, family, colleagues, and even clients that somehow, almost without her realizing it, it's been almost four years since she's been in any sort of serious relationship. She says she just keeps dating the wrong type of guy.

Serially Unlucky or Serially Unfocused?

As Nicole starts talking in detail about Jake, Kevin, and Dom—the last three guys in her life—it becomes clear that although they all sound different on the surface (one was an Australian craftsman, one was a soccer coach from Texas, and the other a cop from her hometown), each guy had recently come out of a long-term relationship when he met Nicole. "That's what I mean. I'm just unlucky when it comes to dating!" says Nicole. "What are the chances that I just keep meeting men who've just come out of bad marriages, had their girlfriends cheat on them, or some other drama like that? I always seem to get them when any sort of commitment is the last thing that they are interested in."

Is Nicole just really unlucky, or could she be partly to blame? While I'm not suggesting that it's entirely her fault (blame is not the goal here; getting what you want is), when I asked her if she thinks there's a pattern to the type of men she's falling for, Nicole draws a blank. "No! These are the men I'm just naturally attracted to and who are attracted to me. You know how it is—it's something that's out of my control. I'm just praying it changes by the time I'm ready to get married!"

What sort of men we date is a lot more important than most of us realize. I don't know about you, but until I started my arranged-marriage interviews, I just dated based on who came my way, seemed fun, and looked cute. There's nothing wrong with having fun and experimenting, but here's the thing: the men we date turn into the men we marry. It's that simple. Why do you think Victorian families (think Jane Austen here) so carefully controlled the suitors their daughters met and even danced with? Why do you suppose wealthy families used to—and in many cases still do—take their daughters to debutante balls to meet young men of the same background?

It's romantic to believe we can date rock stars, starving artists, and playboys and then one day magically fall in love with a nice guy who wants to settle down and raise a family. But is it realistic? I don't think so. If you want to get married, you have to take a close look at the last few men you dated. How would you feel about marrying any of them?

Deciding on the man you will marry is easily one of—if not

the—biggest life decisions that you'll ever make. It influences virtually every aspect of your future life, including where and how you will live, raise your family, spend your free time and money, and evolve as a person. For better or worse, it's also one of the biggest influencers on your day-to-day happiness and habits.

If that's the case, then why do most of us actually put more research, planning, and rational thought into applying for college, managing our careers, or buying a house than we do into really thinking about the type of man we want to date or marry?

Think about your current or last relationship: Was it the result of conscious actions and thoughts on your part—or random circumstances? (We'll politely leave out the third, and all too common, option: you had a big night out, the beer goggles kicked in, and then—boom!—you find yourself dating some guy you don't remember meeting for the first time.) But here's the reality: if you want to find a true life partner, you have to start thinking strategically and carefully about the men you date and why you're dating them.

What I'd Wish I'd Known

Take a moment to ask yourself what you wish you had known about any of your exes before getting involved in a relationship. Think how much time and suffering you could have saved by asking a few more questions or being a bit more honest about your needs! For even more insight, and to prove you're not the only one who has some regrets, next time you're out with your girlfriends, take a poll of what they wish *they'd* known.

Here is a brief snapshot of some of the answers that came up when I asked this question to a few friends—some married, some single—about what they wished they'd known before getting involved with some men from their present or past.

- "That he was married!"

—Sylvia, 34

- "Phil, a man I dated on and off for almost two years, finally confessed to me that he'd decided that he absolutely couldn't be in a serious or even a committed relationship until he was in his late thirties. So maybe he's almost ready now!"

—Julie, 36

- "That he used to have a drug problem and actually went to rehab for almost half a year!"

—Hannah, 29

- "My ex-boyfriend Trevor actually hid from me how important his religion was to him, and it ultimately became the reason that we broke up."

—Samantha, 42

- "I wish I'd known that the reason I could never meet my ex-boyfriend's family is that he had been estranged from them since college over something he'd done to his younger brother."

—Barbara, 37

If you've never given much thought to the men you date and what a future with them might look like, you're not alone. Many women don't. So here's my question: Why is it that even the most organized and ambitious women are often so reluctant to view our dating lives and relationships with any thought to what we ultimately want in a life partner?

I believe there are two main reasons. The first is that we've been culturally conditioned to romanticize the idea that "real love" should be spontaneous and impulsive. After all, why give love any forethought when we expect Cupid to come down and do the work for us?

The second problem brings us back to all those cultural messages about love that we've been OD-ing on for years. In the last secret we talked about the harm of the Prince Charming myth—the belief that there is one single, solitary soul mate for each of us. Well, there's an even sneakier myth out there: it's the boy-meets-girl-and-they-hate-each-other-but-then-they-discover-they're-really-perfect-for-each-other-and-fall-in-love-and-live-happily-ever-after myth. (Funny how all of the love myths have the same exact ending, don't you think?) For more information on this all too popular myth, see *Pride and Prejudice, Cheers,* and *When Harry Met Sally.*

No wonder the concept of actually analyzing what we need and want from our partners and marriages in the long term and then applying that to our dating lives is completely alien to us. After all, it's the complete opposite of all our Hollywood notions about love and marriage—which, by the way, are totally contradictory. Should we be looking for a feeling of love and passion or a feeling of hatred and annoyance? Or, as another well-known love maxim tells us, love comes when you least expect it—so perhaps we should we not look at all. Which means we should just sit there waiting and hoping while time passes us by, because you can't hurry love. But then, of course, people start to tell us, "You have to put yourself out there." It's enough to drive a person crazy!

What It *Really* Means to Have a Type

Sharon, a bubbly 38-year-old primary school teacher, had agreed with her mother that if another birthday came around and she was still single, she'd try a dating service, "or, as my mother prefers to call it euphemistically, an 'introduction agency'!" Sharon's mother helped her find an agency in Atlanta that came highly recommended from a family friend, and her mom even agreed to foot the fairly substantial registration fee.

Sharon's problems and anxieties started when the agency gave her the match forms to fill out. "It just felt so odd to describe what I was looking for in a potential partner in this sort of abstract way. I mean, I've always been quite proud that, unlike some people, I actually don't have a set type. Once I meet someone I tend to know if I'm attracted to him. Plus, she continued, "it felt wrong to write something down that eliminates a whole type of person that I might like but haven't met yet." And so, still single, Sharon continues to hold out for that person that she can't describe but will just somehow "know."

Here's the problem for both Sharon and the rest of us: We've been so internally conditioned to believe that love should be something that just hits us over the head (or strikes us with lightning), that we feel like we don't need to really *do* anything to find it. But marriage or any long-term relationship isn't about the flowers and intense excitement that comes with initial attraction; it's the day-to-day activities that end up creating a shared life and home. This may not sound as exciting or romantic as spontaneous combustion, but trust me, it's actually better. It's real, it's secure, it's attainable, and it's what makes everyday life pretty amazing.

In her book *Surrendering to Marriage,* author Iris Krasnow describes how the process of finding a partner and building a marriage is essentially like building your own civilization. Marriage is a stitch in an intergenerational story that extends across generations and is a result of a decision and commitment made by two people.

But by consciously and unconsciously failing to acknowledge that marriage isn't actually a two-hour movie, we tend to focus on all the wrong things when it comes to planning our relationship futures. For instance, we focus on finding a certain type of man (rugged, sporty, edgy, rich) and gloss over the really important stuff—like what it will be like to spend every day of our lives with this human being or make big decisions about finance and family with him.

In reality, your type, in the traditional sense of looks or outer personality, means very little when it comes to finding a lifelong mate. I can't tell you how many women I meet in their late thirties, forties, and fifties who have found happiness with men they say they never would have dated when they were younger. Their message: Don't discount a guy because he doesn't fit your description of your perfect, idealized man.

Lydia, 37, is an industrial relations adviser in London. Five years ago, she broke up with her boyfriend of two years. Why? "Bill wasn't right for me. I always thought he was too shy and quiet to really be my type." Since then Lydia has, with an energy I genuinely admire, been dating steadily and seriously. She admits that she is sick of it but insists, "I know that each date I go on is bringing me closer to understanding the type of man I'm really looking for."

But is it really?

Actually, Lydia could easily be dating for another five, ten, or twenty years, adding to what is really just a superficial list of what makes up her type. Unless she's actually thinking about what exactly she is looking for (and not just blindly hoping to "feel" it), the concept of a type doesn't have much real meaning.

Psychologist Gilda Carle, associate professor at Mercy College and author of *Don't Bet on the Prince—How to Have the Man You Want by Betting on Yourself,* says, "We go round and round, and we date some more and we think, yes! We have finally found the secret to landing a perfect mate. And still the divorce rate goes higher and higher."

Your Marriage Musts

When it comes to figuring out the type of partner you're really looking for, it's not about a list of likes and dislikes; it's about getting really honest about yourself, your life, and your future and figuring out your "marriage musts." These musts aren't something you find "out there" or after lots of random dinners and movies out. They are values and lifestyle choices that you determine from "in here"—the sometimes frightening place found deep within yourself.

If this feels weird to you, there's a good reason. I'll bet that no one has ever told you before that your type has more to do with *you* than with the men you meet. And that it's a good idea to be extremely specific about what you're looking for. In fact, to some women this whole concept feels a little creepy. As my friend Carol, a 33-year-old Long Island PR executive, told me when I suggested she create a list of her marriage musts (to help move her away for her pattern of dating troubled musicians on the make, who generally drifted in and out of her life borrowing money, crashing in her apartment, and then leaving her emotionally and financially drained), "that kind of preplanning just sounds so manipulative that I could never do it."

Carol isn't alone in her belief that finding a life partner should not be a matter of strategy and planning. So many of us desperately want to believe in the message sold to us in movies like

Pretty Woman and *Maid in Manhattan*: that love alone is enough to overcome any differences (even between a street hooker or hotel maid and a high-flying executive) that we are willing to suppress our real needs and wants in the name of romance.

And of course, it doesn't help that being a "slave for love" is, ironically, one of the few areas in our society where it's okay to be out of control. From movies to music lyrics, the idea of helpless infatuation and having no choice but to love someone (no matter how unlikely or inappropriate) is constantly being glamorized and held up as a model of real love. Admittedly, it might feel like fun at the time, but it's a terrible way to approach anything long-term, especially something as important as marriage.

It's time to break out of these patterns, ladies! Let's leave behind these ideas and beliefs that have passively held us back until now. I'm going to show you how to start taking charge of your dating and romantic life to find a great partner and live the life you want.

Countless studies have shown the life-changing power of writing down your goals. Bestselling author and personal development guru Anthony Robbins has made the exercise of committing your goals to paper a key part of his programs and seminars. He says: "There's something about writing down your objectives on a piece of paper that makes them real. It takes them from the world of wishes to the first step in creating your new reality." Although experts aren't sure exactly why such a simple act can be so effective, they all agree that simply writing down goals greatly increases your chances of achieving them. One explanation is that the process of putting them down on paper primes your brain to start to scan the environment and be alert to opportunities to make them happen.

While many people use this strategy in business, it is just as effective in personal relationships. It's no surprise that there's a book titled, *Write It Down, Make It Happen!*

In this section, I am going to walk you through the process of determining your marriage musts. This will change the way you approach dating and meeting possible partners, and it can even change and improve a relationship you're currently in. To make it happen, you must determine your musts!

Determining your marriage musts means going beyond the usual clichés of "tall, dark, and handsome" and really being honest about what your personal relationship and life fundamentals are. It means being honest enough to know what you actually want versus what you feel you *should* want or what your friends or parents want you to want. No one else is going to see this list (unless you decide to share it), so don't be ashamed or embarrassed by anything that comes to mind. And along the way, you may be surprised by what you find.

For instance, if having a partner who is really involved in you, the kids, and your family is a real priority, then someone with a well-paid but highly demanding and time-consuming profession may initially seem appealing, but over the long term, may not be as aligned with you and your values. Someone who may make much less money but will have the time and energy to invest in your family life would actually be a better match.

Here's what happened to 31-year-old Angela when she actually thought about the type of life that would make her happy. "I decided not to just rush through doing this list, but actually take the time to think about how I honestly want my life to be." Until then, Angela had always dated and tried to meet "the classic sort of type-A guys who were really academic and really professionally driven, which is quite the opposite of me and what I really like." When she did her marriage musts list, she realized that until then she had been dating the kind of people she felt her parents wanted her to be. "Both my parents are devoted to their careers, but I'm more of work-to-live type person. But I hadn't allowed myself to find someone that I could relax around and be more myself with."

Imagine for a moment that you are going to buy your dream apartment or house. You're excited! You can't wait for it to be yours and you can already picture what life in it will be like. So you hire a real estate agent, telling her, "I'm ready. Find me my dream place! I can't tell you right now for sure what my budget is, or how many rooms I really want, or actually even the neighborhood where I want to live. But don't worry; just show me the places since I know I'll recognize it as soon as I walk in."

Obviously that would be completely ridiculous. But that's exactly what many women do when it comes to relationships.

If you have been like me or most of the singles I know, you never specifically clarified what you were looking for in a husband. There was always an assumption that somehow we would "just know" when we met the right person and then everything else would just smoothly fall into place after that.

I'm telling you now that based on everything I learned from both my interviews and my own experiences, the absolute best thing you can do for yourself, your love life, and your future is to just let that assumption go.

This next part is so important that you need to put down the book for a minute, go and get yourself a pen, your laptop, your BlackBerry, anything, and make sure you do more than just read over the questions below. This exercise could literally change your life. It did mine.

Determining Your Marriage Musts

Step One: Figure Out What You *Don't* Want
Core values are at the heart of truly knowing your needs. JoAnne White, a therapist and instructor at Temple University, explains: "These are the things about yourself that are not likely to change. They are the tenets you grew up believing and that deep down

inside still seem to fit into your life no matter what else changes. And while we have all heard that opposites attract, when it comes to really big issues in our life, shared values are what count the most."

An easy way to begin figuring out what you want is to list what you don't want. Often a trip down memory lane past old dates and relationships can provide an incredibly rich (and perhaps slightly depressing) sense of where and with whom you've been in the past and what you know you don't want again.

In this step, in your journal or on a scrap of paper, list all of the traits you *don't* want in a mate: for example, doesn't want children, has a bad temper, doesn't believe women should work after marriage, takes lots of risks, isn't spiritual, not close with his family, drinks a lot, works long hours, is dishonest—you get the idea.

Step Two: Get Clear on What You *Do* Want

The questions below are designed to spark your thinking about what values and characteristics are most important to you in a mate.

Note: It's important that you don't interpret these marriage musts as meaning that the person has to have *all* of these qualities or traits right now. What I learned from studying arranged marriages is that it's more important to look at a person's fundamental qualities and potential that will develop over time. This is not about instant gratification. Often, a person may not be there yet, but may be on the path to developing or creating your musts. Or the musts may come packaged in a slightly different way than you expected, which is why understanding the core result is essential: so you don't miss out on an opportunity.

Telling the difference can sometimes be tough, but when you are clear on what you are looking for, it does get easier. In arranged marriages, for instance, families often look to other relationships a potential mate has had to get a sense of where certain traits will lead. This is one of the reasons that matchmaking in an arranged marriage tends to be such a collective effort.

That was the case with Eun Mi, a 29-year-old software developer from Korea. "Even though I had lived in the United States for almost five years, I knew that I wanted to marry someone who spoke Korean and was interested in the country and culture," says Mi. As a result, she just assumed that she would end up with a man of Korean descent. But luckily she was clear that her "must" was that her mate be interested in her country; he didn't necessarily have to be Korean. "I met Carlos at my favorite Korean bakery where I would always see him on Saturday mornings," says Eun Mi. Carlos was not Korean, but he was fluent in the language, had lived there for five years and actually taught international relations (with a focus on Asia!) at the local college.

Eun Mi's story shows why you need to be very, very clear and very, very honest with yourself about your marriage musts (remember, no one else ever needs to see your list!). If Eun Mi had genuinely wanted to meet a man of Korean descent, she might have been disappointed with Carlos in the future, perhaps when they had children. Or, if she had said she wanted a Korean— rather than narrowing in on the fact that she wanted someone interested in Korean culture—she might have discounted Carlos unnecessarily.

Here are some questions to help you determine what your specific musts for a husband actually are. Remember to write down your answers.

- What things are most important to him in life (family, money, career success, justice, self-actualization, religion, social status, animal rights, serving his country)?
- What kind of career and future career prospects does he have (desire to run his own business, future in a family business, ar-

tistic or creative goals, international work, a secure corporate future, happy to be a stay-at-home dad so you can focus on your career, doesn't matter to you at all)?

- What kind of education does he have? Is he intellectually curious?
- What roles do you see each of you playing in your family and career lives?
- Where has he lived? Where does he want to live? What kind of lifestyle do you picture having (urban, country, lots of travel)?
- What activities is he involved with (community activities, a country club, raising kids, jetting to Paris)?
- Does he drink, smoke, take drugs? How much?
- How important are religion and spirituality to him?
- How important is family to him? Is he close to his? Does he have children already? Does he want children in the future?
- What kind of family background does he come from? What is his relationship with his family?
- What are his politics? How important are his political views to him?
- What age group does he fall into?
- What else is essential to you in a life partner?

Step Three: Decide Who *You* Must Be to Attract This Person

Look over the list of marriage musts you've created and then write down what sort of person *you* would have to be to meet, attract, and sustain the interest of this type of person. Or put it this way: what do you think the man who meets *your* marriage musts list would be putting on *his* marriage musts list?

This is a step most women leave out when looking for a mate, but it's a very important component of the arranged-marriage process: making sure that the woman has the right qualities to interest the sort of man her family hopes for her to marry. In

India a generation ago, families would send their daughters to English convent schools because it was thought to lead to better husband matches!

So ask yourself, is there anything you need to examine in yourself to attract the kind of person you really want?

Very important: This does not—repeat, *does not*—mean becoming someone you're not or becoming a new person. After all, most likely you also exhibit many similar or complementary characteristics to the ones you listed in your ideal mate, which is why you are attracted to such a person. This step is more a matter of figuring out how to cultivate, leverage, and showcase these aspects of yourself so you are more likely to attract a man with the qualities you desire.

Marketing matters. Rachel Greenwald, bestselling author of *Find a Husband After 35 Using What I Learned at Harvard Business School,* created what she calls "the Program" to help women learn to present themselves in the best and most efficient way to find themselves a husband based on marketing tactics that she learned while getting her M.B.A. The Program is a fifteen-step action plan to finding a husband; it takes the view that the reader is the "product" that needs a "strategic plan" to help present itself. Step five, for instance, is "Branding: Identify What Makes You Different," and step six is "Advertising: Promote Your Personal Brand."

Similarly, once you realize what your marriage musts actually are, you often realize that the way you have been presenting yourself might not reflect who *you* really are. This could be the reason why you aren't meeting the type of men or having the quality of relationship that you want.

That was the problem that 29-year-old Erin had. Growing up in Aspen, Colorado, right in the Rockies, she is a classic ski bunny. Most weekends found her on the slopes and then at the bars afterward. "All through high school and college I was known as a real party chick, and, to be honest, I liked it. I always had lots of boyfriends and had a really good time!" What Erin noticed over the past three years is that she was still meeting the same kind of guys that she had met in college: guys who thought of her as the good-time girl who was happy to drink beer out of a plastic cup in the backyard of someone's house, watching the guys goof around, just like they had for years. But Erin had grown up and was no longer interested in that scene.

"When I did my marriage musts list I realized why I wasn't meeting the kind of guys I wanted. On my list were things like a person interested in community activism"—Erin is quite active in a local organization focused on involving more women in politics—"and family, but whenever I was with guys, I never talked about anything like that; I just reverted back to my old party girl image, since I thought that was the only thing that they would find attractive." By clarifying what she actually wanted from her next relationship, Erin realized that unless she started showing a different side of herself, she was never going to meet a man who wanted to share those things with her.

In essence, my message is to be the person you're looking for. Focus on living a life and making choices based on your most important values and passions, and you will attract a man who shares those musts with you.

Next Steps

Simply by creating a marriage musts list you have taken action. It may not feel like it, but knowing who you are looking for will make it easier to recognize this person when you meet him. This also means you can be proactive and figure out where and how you can encounter more men who meet your criteria: can this can be done through your current circle of friends, or do you need to expand your networks and social activities?

I know from personal experience that there is a real power in becoming attuned to your marriage musts. It's almost as though by clarifying what it is you want and why you want it you suddenly start noticing and attracting people who fit those criteria. For me the process started on January 1, 2003. Our family has a New Year's Day tradition of brunch and resolutions. It's something that my father takes really seriously, diligently committing each of our resolutions into a special leather notebook that he uses just for that purpose. If we happen not to be home that year, he harasses us to e-mail our resolutions so he can write them down with his fountain pen and keep it all consistent! Unhappy with my job at the time, I was thinking about taking a year off, but I wasn't sure what to do, and my dad suggested (only half kiddingly) that I use that time to get married. Although I didn't admit it to him, I wasn't against the idea. I was tired of dating people I had no real interest in or future with. I thought of it as treading-water dating. So I made a list of my marriage musts, really thinking about all the qualities that a man I would marry should have, with a couple of lines on why I wanted each quality. For instance, I had moved so much growing up (almost every four years), and had lived everywhere from Switzerland to the Middle East and South America, so it was really important that I marry someone who had lived and, ideally, studied outside of North America. But since I knew I ultimately wanted to move back to Canada, I wanted someone who was also Canadian and shared an interest in the Canadian political process.

It was a fairly detailed list, and almost instantly it did two things: It really made me realize how wrong the men I was involved with were. And it gave me a clear sense of who this man I would marry would be and where I would be most likely to meet him.

My story is not unique. Many other women I interviewed for this book had similar stories. Victoria, a boutique owner in Los

Angeles, wrote up her list of marriage musts around her thirtieth birthday. "I'd had a lot of fun dating up to that point, but I really wanted to meet someone I could build a shared life with. My mom had a friend who wrote down everything she wanted in a husband and then met a guy, so one day I got on my computer and started typing a description of the man I hoped to meet. I wanted him to be intelligent, witty, someone who wanted children, supportive of my career, and someone I'd enjoy talking to—not the silent type, you know? I like to talk! I even included the pretty specific fact that my dream is to have two homes someday—one in the fast-paced city and one as a relaxing getaway in the country."

Victoria then put up a profile on an online dating site. "It was so easy to look through the guys on the site and ignore the ones who didn't appear to meet the things on my list." About six weeks after she wrote her list, she was contacted on the dating site by a marketing executive named Kevin. On their first date, it was almost uncanny how much Kevin seemed to meet her criteria. "It wasn't love at first sight or anything," says Victoria, "but about halfway through that first date I started to realize he was everything I was looking for. I loved talking to him, he mentioned wanting a family, and he loved hearing about my shop. The relationship just grew from there, and believe it or not we are now engaged, live together in the city, and just purchased a country home! It's amazing to me how important that list was."

Remember that knowing your marriage musts is not about instant screening, but about knowing your criteria before you get caught up in a relationship. As Victoria's story demonstrates, it's also about being able to easily recognize a person who fits what you're looking for. Five months after I wrote out my own list, I met my now-husband at a friend's party. Since I'd done my list, I knew what I was looking for, and once we started talking I had a sense that he could be it. I asked around about him (and of course Googled him). At the time, he was living in London and I was in Toronto. On the pretence of looking for some professional advice I contacted him, and we started exchanging e-mails. It was five months before I saw him again, but the e-mails really allowed me to confirm that he did meet my marriage musts and that this was something I should close on. Which is why, when I next saw him, literally the seventh time we met in person, we decided to get engaged.

This may seem impulsive, but I knew he was right for me. He met all of my marriage musts. We were married five months later and now have been happily married for just over four years and have one adorable little boy. And it all really started that one cold morning, with my New Year's Day hangover, a plate of waffles, a notepad, and a list of marriage musts.

The Just for Now Syndrome: "But I Never Intended for Us to Get Serious!"

Since so many of us don't think about what it is that we really want from a relationship ahead of time, we are left to just go with the flow and become entangled in default relationships with whomever we are dating or attracted to at a given time. I call this being a victim of "just for now" syndrome (and I should know because I suffered from this syndrome more than a few times myself).

A fairly dramatic example of the dangers of just for now syndrome occurred at the engagement party of Ken and Julie. Ken, a 32-year-old struggling writer, and Julie, a 31-year-old Ph.D. student at the University of Pennsylvania, started out as a casual hookup after a run-in at a friend's party. That encounter led to the discovery that they both lived in the same apartment building, just a few floors apart. This geographical convenience meant that they started to see each other on a more regular basis.

"Ken was cute and I was attracted to him, but I never intended to get serious or even really involved," Julie recalls, looking back. "He was just someone fun who was there, and around at funny hours when I was lonely after struggling with my thesis for most of the evening." A year later, when his apartment lease was suddenly terminated, he asked Julie if he could move in. "It was supposed to be just for a few months," Julie explains, "but I hadn't had a relationship in over a year and he was single too. I started to get romantic and wonder if maybe we weren't meant to be something more." Julie's sister, who met Ken when she came to stay in Philadelphia for a couple of weeks, was unimpressed with him and concerned by the way Julie seemed to be passively defaulting into this relationship.

"She probably wouldn't have been so concerned if she didn't think Ken was so completely different than me and the kinds of people I enjoyed spending time with. I've always been more of a homebody; I'm quite shy, and I guess you could say that I've always been pretty serious about school, my career, and just my whole life. Ken was, and probably still is, a big party guy. He used to smoke a lot of pot, drink almost every night, and even though he talked a lot about writing, he didn't seem to actually get that much done."

Eight months after he had "temporarily" moved in, Julie had made a nice dinner to celebrate a job offer she'd gotten, after which, Ken proposed. Stunned, Julie accepted. At first they were both caught up in the excitement of it. "Planning the wedding probably kept us together an extra few months since we both got really into it," she remembers sadly.

Although her family wasn't thrilled and refused to believe that Julie would want the kind of life she would have with Ken, she was adamant. "I get tired just thinking about it now. I started to try and help Ken in any way I could. I mean, he was going to be my husband!" Help involved writing his résumé for him and trying to suggest jobs other than the pizza place where he was "temporarily" working, just till he finished his first novel. It meant getting course catalogs from local colleges and trying to figure out how many credits he needed to finish his degree.

Julie finally ended the relationship a few months after their engagement party. "I was sitting there, all dressed up and listening to Ken give a toast about how he should thank the landlord for kicking him out for not paying his rent, since now he won't have to ever worry about rent money again. I knew it was a joke, but hearing it was like being hit in the face. I suddenly jolted awake and thought, How did I end up in this situation? It still scares me to think that I came that close to marrying him."

In a 2003 *Psychology Today* article, Cathy Surra, who teaches at the University of Texas, distinguishes between "event-driven" and "relationship-driven" courtships. According to her research, a match like Ken and Julie's that escalates based on external factors that have little to do with a couple's true level of intimacy— such as moving in together to save money—can be described as event-driven. People in these situations report being far more conflicted and uncertain about their relationships.

Beware the Wedding Industrial Complex

Anne Kingston, author of *The Meaning of Wife*, coined the term "the wedding-industrial complex" to describe what underpins the bridal lust that drives women like Julie to become so focused on the wedding day that they begin to overlook the bigger picture: the type of life they are committing to, not the dress and the ceremony. Basically, they forget that being a bride leads to being a wife.

Kingston argues, "If ever an industry was actively designed to create tenuous marriages based on unrealistic expectations, it would look just like the wedding industrial complex," a machine that Kingston says is fueled by the profit motive and lubricated by myth. It includes magazines, books, retailers, websites, jewelers, dress manufacturers, wedding show organizers, and even the marketers who create advertisements for such products as ice cream and cigarettes. "This has shifted the cultural focus to making the wedding the exclusive focus, with the marriage as the afterthought."

Perhaps you're starting to think I go around telling 12-year-old girls to date only boys who meet their marriage musts. Or that I would discourage college girls from having some fun and dating a few different kinds of guys. I promise you I'm not! And I wouldn't! I certainly didn't do that. After all, no one wants *always* to be focused on the long term or on marriage, especially when it's just a causal date or an occasional hookup with some really hot guy!

But this book is for women like you, who are either done with that or don't want that and instead want to meet a real partner and build a life together. If marriage is what you want, unless you are really clear on your marriage musts (which most women *aren't*), there's a good chance that the just for now syndrome will kick in and lead you away from your goals. As Julie found out the hard way, as we get caught up, get comfortable, and form a habit, we can become so much more involved in a relationship than we ever intended. It's easy to understand how things just keep going and time passes.

If you find yourself suffering from just for now syndrome, a part of you might tell yourself that this relationship isn't really right and that soon you'll make a change. But there are two risks to this attitude.

The first is that you are missing out on other, more appropriate or suitable relationship opportunities. The second is that even if you might still be dating other people, you're not really allowing yourself to be open to those possibilities. That's what happened with 34-year-old Christy, who ended up involved with a married colleague from her investment firm. "I was theoretically dating other people, in that I was going out for dinner and drinks with different people, but I wasn't actually open to anything. Even if I wasn't willing to admit it, I just kept hoping Peter would leave his wife to be with me." Aggravating this tendency to wait is that too many women (and men) still confuse good sex with love, especially in the beginning of a relationship.

The second risk associated with just for now syndrome is that it becomes easier and easier to start to overlook and explain away those initial concerns or issues that first made you think that this person wasn't right for the long term. The risk is that you then end up married or seriously involved with this person, although his values and visions are not aligned with your own.

This inevitably results in clashes, distances, disappointments, breakups, or divorce. Studies have found that half of all divorces take place within the first three years of marriage, primarily as a result of people discovering dimensions in their partners that they hadn't anticipated or fully understood. Diane Sollee, founder and director of Smart Marriages, says in a 2003 *Psychology Today* article, "[During] the first two years a couple is essentially creating a civilization, and that's one of the reasons why the divorce rate is highest."

Take Maria, now 34, and Jacob, now 33. The two met when they were both undergraduates at school in Vermont. They were instantly attracted and at ease with one another. Maria was a communications student and Jacob was taking a series of courses but could never quite commit to a major. They dated and lived together for over six years, although Maria admits, "Deep down,

I knew Jacob wasn't really right for me long-term." Eventually, after years together, they married—only to divorce a year and a half later. "Suddenly, things that I'd ignored before started to really bother me, like how boyish he always seemed and how he could never commit professionally to anything. I know he thought that things would just continue on the way they had for the past few years, but I just kept thinking, How could I ever have kids with this man?"

Without clarifying and committing to your marriage musts, you are leaving one of the most important decisions in your life up to chance and circumstance. Don't waste any more time waiting for life to come to you. Decide what you want, get it, and then go about living the rest of your dream life. That's what women in arranged marriages do, and there's no reason you can't follow this strategy.

The Arranged-Marriage Way: Decide What You Want and Go Find It

One of the fundamental purposes of an arranged marriage is to prevent the mistakes that come with infatuation and short-term thinking. Instead, the process is designed to rationally assess the values and characteristics of potential partners in order to determine what type of life the couple will likely lead over the long term.

It usually starts with the individual (much aided and supervised by parents, siblings, and extended family and friends) creating a list of the key requirements or qualities that possible marriage candidates must have. This means that unlike many of our (and certainly my own) past relationships, there is very little randomness to an arranged marriage. Instead, there are clear rules, a definitive set of criteria, and a systematic evaluation and selection process. It might not sound romantic, but it's incredibly practical—which is why it works.

Sonya is 33; she's been married for almost four years and has one son. She and her husband both teach at their local university. She is part of the English faculty and he teaches in the physics department. Sonya, who is of Indian descent, grew up in a small town in Massachusetts where "arranged marriages, brown people, and good Chinese food were all nonexistent!" Like many of the younger, American-born women I spoke with, Sonya admits, "I never would've thought I'd have an arranged marriage. I mean, when I was growing up my younger brother and I would laugh and say that they were only for people who were desperate."

Sonya approached her mother about an arranged marriage when she was about to turn 29. It wasn't that she was desperate, but "I was so tired of dating. I felt like I'd been doing it solidly for twelve years, and I was only meeting guys who couldn't or wouldn't commit, seemed to have addiction or employment issues, or I just could never see fitting in with my family. I was beginning to become jaded and frustrated." She laughs and adds, "So maybe I was actually a *little* desperate!"

It was when Sonya started agreeing to let her colleagues and old school friends set her up on blind dates that her thoughts on arranged marriages started to shift. "It just hit me after one particularly lame blind date that I was letting all these random people essentially filter prospects for me, but I was refusing to let the people who knew me the best and cared about me the most have any say in the process."

Despite the exchange of photographs and occasional meetings, feelings like romantic love or attraction just aren't part of the initial arranged-marriage equation. In fact, throughout my interviews, I continually heard this sort of comment: "When you are young and think you're in love, it's the worst time to pick a spouse, because emotion and hormones are clouding any chance at reason."

I know, I know. The idea of handing over control of such a significant decision to your family probably sounds incredibly unnerving. But arranged marriages are based on the idea that your family will have your best interests at heart and that, often, it's harder to see yourself as you truly are. Our families can know us better than we think we know ourselves. (If you don't have a close relationship with your family and this comment doesn't resonate, think about some other important people in your life, such as longtime friends, roommates, or other relatives who would fit this description.) It's an idea that is increasingly gaining traction, as the success of websites such as matchmakingfriends.com, datemymate.net, and matchmakingmoms.com all show. These are all online dating networks where family and friends—and not the daters—candidly network to find a partner for their loved ones.

"I met my husband once before we got married, when he came to my parents' house for tea, but we only exchanged a few sentences about his new job and my upcoming graduation," says Preeti. Varun, Preeti's husband for the past twenty-seven years, was the result of an eighteen-month search by her family for the right man. "They rejected fifteen other matches," she tells me, still pleased thinking about it. Despite their brief meeting, Preeti describes the relative ease with which she and her husband began their life together, moving to Canada, building a business, and raising two kids. "Varun and I always had a lot to say to each other. Of course we were nervous at first, but I soon found that, growing up, we had read many of the same books, had similar relationships with our siblings, and wanted the same things for our family."

Before (or if) they ever meet, all candidates in an arranged marriage are screened, which means that, generally, by the time a couple is married, all the hard questions in terms of expectations around home, money, health, community, spiritual life, and family have already been considered and addressed. This process is eased by the fact that the couple can readily convey all their concerns or questions through their matchmakers.

Women in Arranged Marriages Share Their Marriage Musts

"I was young when I got married—just eighteen—so my only "must" was that he was taller, but not skinnier, than me! My mother was in charge of the list and they were looking for an educated professional who was at least five to seven years older and from a good family like ours. They found him! My husband is a pediatrician who grew up in a household that sounds like it could have been mine!"

—Nermeen, 52

"I'd dated a bit before, though never anything serious. By the time I decided to have an arranged marriage, I knew exactly what I wanted my parents to look for. What were my marriage musts? Someone who had the same level of education and professional accomplishment as me, who'd lived or studied outside of the United States, who wanted children and was quite involved with his family. . . . I can keep going, it was pretty specific! It worked out really well, and was a real time saver, since my parents screened so many different guys for me. I don't know how it would have been if I'd actually had to date my way through them all!"

—Karine, 39

"My aunt arranged my marriage for me. She asked me along the way what I wanted, and I met some of the prospects, but I trusted her, so I pretty much let her decide.

Her biggest must was that he own his own business so he wouldn't have to depend on someone else for a job."

—Naima, 56

"My parents arranged my marriage and religion was very important to them. It was a must that he be a nondrinker, a nonsmoker, and a complete vegetarian. I wanted someone who was going to live overseas and who would take me traveling a lot. I would say we both basically got what we were looking for."

—Acquila, 59

"We all had a say in what should be on the list—me, my parents, my brother, and my cousins—I think it was quite long, since they wanted to be sure they married me to someone who would support my career and education as well. They had eight candidates lined up, but as soon as my father met my now husband, he canceled everyone else since he was so impressed with him!"

—Laila, 29

London-born Ruby hasn't really ever thought of herself as someone who would have an arranged marriage. In fact, she is probably the opposite of the image that usually comes to mind when you think of an arranged marriage.

Ruby, 35, is the owner of a small independent art gallery in Manhattan. She looks like she just stepped out of a designer boutique's window. With strong, perfectly made-up features and straight black hair that falls to her waist, she's the sort of woman who instantly gets noticed. Over a drink at a small bar down the road from her gallery, she tells me how she ended up deciding on an arranged marriage. "Before I met Sanjay, I kept dating sort of suave European banker or media types. The sort of men you would say were sophisticated." And that's exactly who I would picture her with, I comment. "That was the problem," she agrees. "That's what everyone, including me, pictured me with. But the problem was, I could never really relax with any of them."

Ruby comes from a close middle-class family. "My parents never drink; their lives were about doing well to help us, going to temple, and family time. I guess I never realized how much their values impacted me in terms of what I felt comfortable with—especially as I got older." When Ruby was 32, she decided to have an arranged marriage: "My biological clock was ticking; I wanted babies! But I just didn't see it happening with any of the 'glam' guys I was meeting. I wanted someone stable, a good father and someone I could finally relax with." (We'll look at the role that physical image and style have in confusing your marriage musts in Chapter 4.)

Ruby describes her decision as "liberating." She explains: "For the first time ever, I think, I was really honest about who I actually was and what I wanted: bookish, professional, a non-drinker. Someone who fit with me and wouldn't care or even notice that my parents haven't redecorated a thing in their house since the early 1970s when they first bought it!"

It turns out the process took a bit longer than Ruby thought: the first family that her parents were hoping for didn't feel comfortable with a woman who had a past. (This can be one of the downsides of an arranged marriage: your past life and relationships are often open to the scrutiny and critical commentary of everyone involved. Although as one friend who had an arranged marriage after dating commented, I was kidding myself if I thought that didn't happen with any relationship once it got serious!) But within the year Ruby's family had found someone they felt was right. The families met twice and it was decided.

Sonali opens her wallet and shows me a picture of her husband, Sanjay, a 37-year-old pediatrician whose father actually went to school with Ruby's. A tall, slightly rumpled man in the picture, he's looking adoringly at his glamorous wife and daughter. "Being with Sanjay is really just like coming home," she says.

Using the arranged-marriage approach can work for you. Although the idea of having such a clear and definite list of requirements for a possible spouse may seem restrictive, it actually has several benefits.

The first is that it makes it much easier to think about where to find possible prospects. For example, if, like Ruby, you are looking for a man who enjoys reading, books, and ideas, then maybe instead of spending Thursday evening at your local bar, decide to browse the aisles of Barnes & Noble or attend readings and discussion groups. If you want a man who is religious, you could join a young professionals group at your local church or synagogue. Once you get clear on your marriage musts, it becomes easier to see and find opportunities that could allow you to meet a man who fits your needs.

When I became clear on my marriage musts, I realized that I had one friend who would be just the person to introduce me to the kind of man I was looking for, since those were naturally the type of people she tended to know and have as friends. So I made a point of always attending her parties and dinners, whether I was in the mood or not. And I was right. It was at a drinks party at her house that I met my husband, and it was a party that I would have missed if I hadn't made the decision based from the place of my musts. I'd had the world's worst day at work that Friday, had completely broken out, had a fight with the guy I was dating at the time, and going out was the last thing I wanted to do. But looking back, I'm so glad I did, since Rana was only in town for that weekend, and if I hadn't followed my musts, I could have completely missed meeting him.

The second advantage of the arranged-marriage approach is that by clearly articulating your requirements for a spouse, you'll simultaneously clarify the kind of person *you* have to be or the traits you need to develop or showcase in order to attract this type of person. This means first being honest about what you are really looking for and then thinking about what traits in yourself you need to highlight or develop to attract someone like that. This does not mean being fake; it means emphasizing the parts of yourself that match the man you want to meet.

For instance, if one of your marriage musts is to find someone who is intellectual, then it makes sense to emphasize your own education and intellect as well. Dara, a 36-year-old doctor in Miami, was keen to marry a professional with an international perspective who would also want a large family. So, when describing herself to possible prospects, she made sure to emphasize the close relationship she had with all five of her sisters as well as the fact that she had loved studying in Israel, London, and Madrid.

Carol, a 31-year-old bank auditor from Connecticut, describes her self-insight: "I always wanted to meet someone who was a real activist—very political and involved in making a difference. But when I did my marriage musts, I also realized that I hadn't been involved with anything even remotely like that since my second year of university." Being honest about what she wanted in her marriage helped Carol realize the change she probably needed to make in her own activities and behaviors in order to meet someone who had the qualities she was looking for. In her case, being clear on her marriage musts prompted her to look up the local chapters of charity organizations that she once volunteered for and to start that side of her life again. The obvious bonus of clarifying your marriage musts is that you get closer to your own personal life musts and start living a life that is more authentic and joyful in every way.

In case you aren't convinced and still think that detailing your marriage musts is either a waste of time or something that seems too preplanned, then keep in mind that it's the failure to really know our marriage musts that often leads to one or more of the following problems.

First, when we aren't clear on what we really want from a relationship, we risk, as Maria did by marrying Jacob, wasting years with a person who we know or suspect isn't actually right for us—particularly since, as most of us know, getting into a relationship is often a whole lot easier than getting out of one! Inertia, stability, fear, laziness, guilt: there are any number of reasons that keep us in a relationship even when we know that it's not right for us and that we have no future with the person.

Second, when we don't have a clear idea of what we want, we meet someone, fall head over heels, and then end up explaining or ignoring all the characteristics that make him or her not right for us in the long run. Once the infatuation wears off, we often find ourselves back in the first scenario: either trying to change the other person or biding our time until we eventually end it.

The truth is that even if you don't explicitly acknowledge your marriage musts, they are already affecting how you feel and the decisions you make. Even though we may not consciously be aware of it, we all have our list of marriage musts deeply ingrained in our heads and in our hearts. And while we can ignore or overlook them in the beginning of a relationship, they tend to surface once the relationship evolves.

This results in a third situation, where each person has a set of hidden or undisclosed expectations. Although people may never actually articulate them to themselves or their partners, they nevertheless still become frustrated and resentful when those expectations are not met. This is what happened with Kate and David, who are the sort of couple that leave you feeling either frightened for your own relationship or deeply grateful that you're single.

Although they are barely two years into their marriage, 32-year-old Kate, a human resources worker, is barely able to speak nicely to or about her husband David, a 29-year-old entrepreneur. Instead, her resentment and incredible frustration seem to spill over into even the most innocuous exchange, whether it's about menus over dinner or deciding if the car needs to be filled up. A casual question reveals that she is annoyed and fed up with everything, from his lack of interest in traveling, to what she sees as his lack of ambition for his small catering company, to her belief that he is threatened by her career prospects and university education.

Although Kate initially seems unwilling to admit it, it turns out that she's also angry that she earns more than David: "Not that it stops him from wasting our money on stupid stuff like speakers and upgrades to the car. Meanwhile, we are still trying to save up enough for a down payment on our condo."

Reading this may have you thinking that Kate and David must have jumped into marriage without really knowing each other. Actually, the opposite is true. Although they've been married a relatively short time, they have been together for over ten years and were once (as unbelievable as it seems now) high school sweethearts.

So what's changed? Kate admits that she was aware of all David's traits and future plans, but acknowledges, "I didn't realize that once we married, I would want something—or really someone—different." This is one of the major advantages of arranged marriages, Internet dating, or a matchmaking service: It is much easier to clearly state what your marriage and partner expectations are before you're ever involved and when you don't have to do it face-to-face. This is why it's important to complete the earlier exercise and honestly and clearly state your marriage musts. The tremendous bonus is that you'll bring yourself closer to living your life the way you want *right now,* whether you're married or single.

As Shelly Rachanow, author of *If Women Ran the World, Sh★t Would Get Done,* agrees. "If you've ever spent a string of Friday nights home alone or out with the girls, it may feel like the words 'a few good men' are more than a movie title. But the truth is, there are plenty of men out there who fit your description and one great, empowering, and fun thing to do is to create a list of must-haves for your dream guy. Write your list down, have fun doing it, and keep it handy for easy reference. Consider it your personal Declaration of Independence from all relationships that are less than what you want, deserve, or are worthy of."

The Case for Going Online . . .

There's a reason that so many of us are going online—it works! Clearly stating your marriage musts and finding guys who are in the same place as you is so much easier.

As Sam Yagan, CEO of OkCupid.com, observes, "There's a much more deliberate courtship process online than what you would find at, say, a bar. In a typical situation there, snap judgments are made on very superficial factors and a two-minute conversation, usually covering absolutely nothing, will determine whether this potential relationship takes off."

So if you haven't done it yet, now could be the time! Lavalife's singles and dating expert Lori Miller offers the following advice for singles looking to click:

- **It's all about the opening line.** Having a headline on your profile that is eye-catching and entertaining and really says something about your personality is key to success.

- **Say something!** Be yourself and take the time to write your profile. It you're not being honest and letting other singles see the real you, what's the point? Be up front and honest about who you are and what you're looking for. It's the surest way to find someone who fits with you.

- **Post a photo (or a few) that actually looks like you.** Profiles with photos are eight times more likely to be viewed by other members. It's important to choose photos that actually reflect your looks and personality.

- **Read his profile—every word.** People create profiles for a reason, and careful reading is the only way to know what they are really looking for. Plus you're more likely to get a response if you call out something they wrote or express a common interest.

Lana, an attractive 34-year-old Vancouver lawyer, is a complete believer in the arranged-marriage approach, which she witnessed firsthand through her old university roommate, who is now happily married and has one daughter. "Women used to marry for love, and with the way things used to be, it was very often their first love. But now, if you've gone to university, and maybe grad school, and you want to concentrate on your career and gain some financial independence, by the time you want to look for a husband you've probably been through three or four serious relationships that haven't worked out.

"I think that's when you start to realize that finding a partner isn't all about falling in love; it's actually about choosing the right man for you, a man with plans for the future that work with yours, who is going to suit your lifestyle and be a good father to your kids rather than just someone who's really good-looking or sexy."

When we spoke, Lana had recently broken up with a man

she had been very much in love with at the start of their relationship. But over the two years they were together, he became very dependent on her, not just financially but emotionally. The inequality of their relationship eventually caused it to collapse.

"I'm at an age and life stage now where, hopefully, the next man I get involved with will be the man I marry and have a family with—and that makes me really nervous! It means that I've stopped thinking in terms of 'the one.' Instead, I'm trying to think about what his prospects are and whether he would be a good match for me." I have no doubt that she'll find her match soon. The marriage musts are magical.

What This Means for You

I can't emphasize enough the transformative power of writing out your marriage musts. There are only a couple of exercises in this book, and this one is far and away the most important and the one that will have the most impact. It's not good enough to just read this chapter: you absolutely have to take the time to let yourself think about the questions, picture your future, and then *write it all down.* If you haven't written out your musts, go back and do it now! In addition to all of the other benefits of writing them down, the process of clarifying what you want in a life partner will start to change the way you approach the entire issue of marriage. You'll start to view marriage in a way that is similar to women in arranged marriages.

People in arranged marriages treat marriage strategically and purposefully; they approach it like the serious long-term decision that it is. In contrast, many of us tend to have a "go with the flow" attitude that is supported by our short-term thinking and desire for instant gratification. Doing your marriage musts will help change this, by prompting you to think long-term about the type of future and family you want to create. My idea of a long-term view to my dating and love life used to be thinking and planning till the end of the weekend! Trust me; the marriage must list worked for me.

Whether you share your marriage musts with close friends, or use them to form the basis of a dating website profile, or share them with a professional dating agency, you will immediately improve your chances of finding a strong match. Even if you decide to keep your marriage musts to yourself, remember to keep them in a place where you can see them and check in with them on a regular basis. Remember, when it comes to meeting a husband, the musts are all that matter.

Living This Lesson

- **Realize that the men you date become the men you marry.** If you're serious about meeting a life partner, get serious about deciding whom to date. Choosing a husband is one of the biggest decisions that you'll ever make, and dating is the first step to that decision. Don't be shy about approaching and treating it as a strategic process.

- **Write down your marriage musts and stick to them.** Unfortunately, love doesn't conquer all in the long term, so know your marriage musts and respect their importance. That means knowing who you have to be and where you have to go to meet your ideal match. The big bonus is that by getting clear on your own values and passions, you'll start to live a more authentic, satisfying life right now.

- **Beware of the "just for now" syndrome.** If you're not careful, you may fall into a so-so relationship and end up married to a man you know isn't a good match. Breaking up with someone who doesn't meet your musts is a lot better than living with the consequences of marrying him.

Chapter Three

Secret #3

Commitment Is
the Opposite of Constraint

Overcoming the One Foot Out the Door Syndrome

Kelly is a 33-year-old veterinarian who recently started dating an old classmate of hers from college. "Gary and I met about four months ago at an alumni event. We had a great time talking and laughing that night, and a few days later he called and asked me out to dinner. For me, things have moved pretty fast since then. Last month we had the 'Are we exclusive?' conversation." Usually, when people are in month four of dating and it seems to be going well, they are giddy with loved-up excitement and bliss. Not Kelly.

"I like Gary, probably more than anyone I've met in the last two years. But then, I liked my last two boyfriends as well and— because of me—those relationships didn't end up working out." Not naturally a pessimistic person, Kelly admits that she's become aware of her own inability to commit. "At first I thought it was funny, a good thing, but now, I'm starting to wonder. It's like, I meet someone, it's going well, but as soon as it starts to get serious or any kind of issues come up, I either end it or do something that pushes the guy to end it. And to be honest, I'm not sure why."

While she admits that this time, with Gary, she hasn't done anything to sabotage the relationship, she says she feels her commitment phobia emerging. "I notice that the more he starts to get serious or wants to share his problems and life with me, the more I start noticing and wanting to go meet other guys. If it was just something I felt with Gary, I wouldn't be so worried, but I've been down this road so many times now that I'm starting to notice a pattern. It scares me. At this rate, where will I end up?"

Kelly is suffering from what I like to call "one foot out the door" syndrome. This is when couples—usually without wanting to or realizing how it happened—end up being only partially committed to each other and the relationship.

Unless you've just returned from a decade-long trip to Mars, our societal lack of commitment to relationships and marriage shouldn't be all that surprising to you. After all, stories of divorce and separation literally surround us, from the covers of *People* magazine and *Us Weekly* to the lives of our own family and friends. For years the U.S. divorce rate has hovered around 50 percent. This statistic doesn't even include all the cohabiting couples, who have an even higher rate of separation. No wonder believing in a stable, happy, and lasting marriage can seem like a naïve fantasy!

Without our even realizing it, this environment of relationship negativity has collectively affected our own behavior and expectations. It's made worse by the fact that so many of us have memories of our own parents or our friends' parents divorcing, remarrying, and then very often divorcing again. Add in our personal experiences of heartbreaks and breakups, and it's no wonder that getting out or getting ready to get out of a relationship often feels much more natural and normal than staying in a relationship for the long term.

Jill, a 29-year-old law student in Boston, was engaged for two years to Tom, a fellow student. Tom ended up breaking the engagement for what she describes as "her attitude" and what he called "her issues." Jill explains: "Tom said he couldn't take my 'cynical little comments' about how the wedding seemed like a waste of money, because had he missed where the divorce rate was? Or my wondering about whether we could still be friends if our relationship ended." Hardly the sound of the hopeful bride! But as Jill explains it, "Both my parents are twice-divorced and I realized that I just can't take the idea of 'forever and ever' seriously. I wish I could, but I just can't."

Gemma Ladden, a family lawyer and partner at Ladden & Allen Chartered in Chicago, has seen the impact of the cases she's worked on. "After decades of raising the children of divorce, we have given birth to a generation with few role models for a long and happy marriage. The unintended consequence of divorce is that our offspring feel their hearts and finances are only safe if they remain committed to being uncommitted."

As depressing as it sounds, Jill's problem is not unique. All of us on some level are far too keenly aware of the possibility that our own relationships and marriages may not last. The result: an epidemic of partial commitment.

The Epidemic of Partial Commitment

By partial commitment, I mean that although we may genuinely care for our partners, enjoy their company, and talk about or plan a future with them, nevertheless, either consciously or unconsciously, we keep one sneaky foot propping open the door of our hearts, our minds, and ultimately our relationship options.

Most of the time, we don't even acknowledge (probably because we don't notice!) how this epidemic is affecting us. Instead, we tell ourselves that we're just being practical when we think about our "plan B," or that it's only natural to wonder if we could do better then our current boyfriend or partner, or what life with a new person would be like, or—well, you know what I mean.

Regardless of how we might rationalize or describe it, this "one foot out the door" state of mind constantly reinforces an environment of partial commitment. And over time this environment wears away at the very foundation of our relationship by preventing us from being fully present to our partner and a full participant in the relationship. And with each such relationship we have, this process becomes faster and more destructive.

Does this feeling sound familiar? Does it describe how you are in your relationships? If it does, then for you this really is one of the most important lessons of this book: by keeping one foot out the door of your relationship, you might think you are protecting yourself from potential disappointment or heartbreak, but you are also keeping yourself from happiness. If you never fully commit to a relationship, you are never fully able to enjoy the fruits of a good relationship: shared joy, a sense of security, and fulfillment.

Plus, if you experience too many bad relationships, then relationship failure starts to feel more normal to you than relationship success. As with Kate, you start feeling weird, unhappy, or uncomfortable when you are in a potentially great relationship because you're so used to the feeling of failure. It's a vicious cycle and a terrible fate!

Partial commitment can manifest itself in any number of ways. Take Maggie, a securities lawyer who hates her job, but (despite regular encouragement from her husband) is too scared to follow her dream of opening a restaurant. "Even after three years of marriage," she says, "I don't want to be financially dependent on Paul, even temporarily, because what if he left? I need the security of a lucrative career, even if I don't love it, but at least it makes me feel that I would still be okay without him."

Twice-married Cynthia, an incredibly fit 42-year-old, admits that she sees her five-times-a-week gym habit as part of her "safety and investment plan for the future. I just feel better knowing that if something goes wrong between Rick and me, other men will still find me attractive."

You may not want to admit it, but pause right now and see if you have any similarities to Maggie and Cynthia. Have you ever (in a current or past relationship) . . .

- Cheated?
- Fantasized about another man when you were having problems (or not!) with your current partner?
- Thought about what you'd do if and when you became single again?
- Developed a contingency plan in case this relationship should fail?
- Secretly checked out an online dating site while in a committed relationship?
- Used words or had thoughts that suggested a relationship was temporary?
- Bad-mouthed your commitment to your partner, marriage, or relationship when you were out with certain people?

This last one was a problem for Rachel, 31, a journalist who's been living with her boyfriend, Ian, for four years. "I had a group of close friends from college that I used to regularly meet for drinks. When I was the first of the group to move in with my boyfriend, I stopped being around nearly as much for our drunken nights out. To be honest, I didn't miss them at all and was glad to have moved on. I love being in a strong and committed relationship, and I love my Ian, but I still find that whenever I'm back with those people, I start putting down my relationship. I make it seem that even though we've been together for four years (and

I actually hope we'll be together for a lot more), I talk about it like it's really a "just for now" type thing. Or that I would be open to being with someone else. Or that I miss being single. None of this is true at all, but I find after a couple of drinks and when I'm around them, I always start talking like that."

Rachel says she's happy with Ian, and talking to her, it's clear that she is. So what would make her undermine and essentially insult herself, Ian, and their relationship the way she does? Well, I think a large part of it is that the general environment of our society is actually not very supportive of couples, relationships, or commitment—even though most single people I know spend large parts of their time and energy looking not to be single. Think of the popularity of such TV shows as *Friends* and *Sex and the City.* They basically end when the characters stop being single! The same goes for chick lit: the story is about the single girl looking for a man. When she finds him and starts a relationship, the story ends and we move on to the next single-gal saga.

The dating world is tough, and even though we would love to believe that our friends are genuinely happy when our dating lives are coming together and working for us, the sad truth is that often our single friends, like Rachel's, want to bring us back into their fold. This isn't necessarily done intentionally, but often occurs just because single friends don't want to lose you to the new man in your life.

It's a predicament that Bridget Jones, the original single girl for our time, observed in her diary:

> "Are you in love?" asked Tom in a suspicious, jealous tone. He's always like this. It's not that he wants to be with me, because obviously he is a homosexual. But if you are single the last thing you want is your best friend forming a functional relationship with someone else.

It doesn't take a Ph.D. in psychology to figure out that regularly putting yourself in situations with unsupportive friends isn't good for your commitment or your happiness!

The "Something Better" Syndrome

Hand in hand with one foot out the door syndrome is the "something better" syndrome. It is practically the American way to believe we can always strive to do better in all area of our lives, even relationships.

We live in a culture of aspiration, self-help, and self-improvement. In many ways, this is one of our best cultural traits—the belief if that if we want something enough and we work hard enough, then we can improve ourselves and our lives. The downside to this belief is that it can also leave us continually feeling dissatisfied and wondering whether we could be happier, do better, or have an easier time—in this case, with another person. When there's always something better to strive for, how can we know when it's okay to stop and enjoy what we actually have?

It was this feeling that ultimately ruined Alice's last real relationship. Alice and Sebastian met at his company's Christmas party. At the time, Alice was working as a chef for the company that had catered the party at Sebastian's accounting firm.

Although it's been over two years since they broke up, Alice, 33, still appears sad when she talks about it. She shows me a picture of the two of them together at a friend's barbecue. Sebastian is a tall, dark-haired man with a friendly expression. In the picture he has his arm around a bare-shouldered Alice and he is smiling down at her.

When they met, he was in the middle of his training to be a CPA. A self-made man, Sebastian left home at 16 and worked to put himself through night school. He and Alice started dating soon after the Christmas party, and by the end of that year; they had rented an apartment in Albuquerque together. "Something happened when we moved in together," Alice recalls wistfully. "I started to compare him to my sisters' husbands and my friends' boyfriends, and, somehow, he always seemed to be wanting. I kept wondering if I was just settling with him, thinking that maybe I could do better."

Alice admits that what constituted "doing better" kept changing depending on the situation (and by the sound of it, what types of guys her friends and colleagues were dating at the time). She becomes vague as she tries to explain what she was thinking at the time. "Oh, I don't know, maybe a little less serious? Sebastian could be pretty intense about things. . . . Or maybe better looking?" Her voice trails off as she struggles to reach for specifics.

Not surprisingly, Sebastian got tired of always coming up short . . . and by the end of the next year, he had moved out. Alice recently heard that he had gotten married and is now on the partner track at one of the big accounting firms in the city. "Looking back, especially now that I've been out there trying to find something better, I realize that there was nothing actually wrong with Sebastian, or our relationship. Really, it was all my own issues and in my own mind."

Something better syndrome is exacerbated by our disposable culture. The attitude that we take to tossing a computer when it stops working, easily leaving a job when another "better" one comes along, and even tossing a perfectly good dress in the trash all contribute to our ability to view relationships as transitional, disposable, and easily replaced. As Monique Chapman, radio host and author of *Getting Your M and M's: The Men and Money Book,* describes it, "We live in a 'drive thru' society today. We want everything right now and are always searching for the next best thing. The media has sold the public the concept of throw-away relationships, that if we don't receive immediate gratification, we move on."

Well, as women in arranged marriages know, good relationships are not so easy to find, and when you find one, you should cherish it.

No Longer Living in Sin, but Is It Living Smart?

The complete opposite of the arranged-marriage approach to marrying someone after a few brief meetings involves "testing the waters" by living with a potential life partner before you commit to marriage. No longer an alternative lifestyle choice, this situation has become almost a life stage for many us (particularly with city rents going higher and higher!). I've heard more than a few people assert that it would be crazy to get married without at least sharing a bathroom first.

But is it?

Nearly 5 million opposite-sex couples in the United States live together outside of marriage, with millions more having done it at some point. And more than 50 percent of couples who marry today have lived together beforehand. (Note: At least 600,000 same-sex couples also cohabit, but their situation is different since most don't have the choice to marry.) Does living together lead to more committed, happier, long-term relationships?

Well, not really. According to a 2003 *Psychology Today* article that focuses on research from Penn State, couples who move in together before marriage have a higher divorce rate and a higher level of discontent in their married life compared to couples who'd been living separately before tying the knot. They are less enthusiastic about marriage and more tolerant of divorce.

As well, couples who move in together before marriage have up to two times the odds of divorce, as compared with couples who marry before living together.

Why is this?

Well, part of it is that previous research has shown that people who already hold a dim view of marriage are more likely to co-habit. But the Penn State study also suggests that the act of living together leads to a more negative view of marriage. Authors William Axinn and Jennifer Barner propose several theories that might account for this phenomenon. Among them: couples tend to adopt the values and beliefs of the people around them, so two people with concerns or worries about marriage may confirm each other's views.

This begs the question: Why are the precautions that we're taking to ensure marriage is right for us actually working against us? And, given this information, should women seeking happy marriages avoid cohabitation?

While I'm not here to advocate for or against cohabitation (after all, I've done it twice myself, although both times it ended in breakups), but I can tell you that it is not part of the arranged-marriage process. Below is a list of some of the contributing factors working against couples living together before marriage, all of which the arranged-marriage approach is specifically designed to prevent. If you've been living with your partners and it hasn't turned into lasting love or marriage, you might want to think about these factors and try the arranged-marriage approach instead:

- **Living together often results in a "slide" into marriage.** The couple never actually makes the conscious and explicit decision to commit. Instead, you move in, it's comfortable, and soon, even if the relationship isn't right, marriage just starts to seem inevitable—especially once the family pressure kicks in!

- **Couples often end up living together by accident.** Possessions just sort of drift over and then the couple justify the situation because they are spending so much time together anyway. But again, no conscious commitment decision is ever made.

- **The experience of living together can make marriage seem less sacrosanct.** What's special about getting married if you have virtually the same benefits as a cohabiting couple?

Ultimately, living together means only partial commitment. By this, I mean that we are more likely to have different or lower standards when it comes to whom we live with versus whom we marry. It's too easy not to work at the relationship if there are issues because there is always an exit. This applies to the guys as well. A 2004 national study by psychologist Scott Stanley, director of the Center for Marital and Family Studies at the University of Denver, found that men who had lived with their spouses before marriage were on average less committed to their marriage than those who hadn't.

Living together also prolongs the partial-commitment epidemic, since it often seems like a good way to share expenses, have some companionship, and feel more secure without a great deal of obligation. But, as I pointed out earlier, by doing this, women are not protecting themselves; instead they're actually denying themselves many of the wonderful aspects of fully committed relationships.

Keep all of this in mind the next time you are tempted to leave your toothbrush and a few changes of clothes at your boyfriend's place, in the hopes that it will gradually turn into something more!

Ditch Your Plan B

Perhaps you're feeling a bit defensive right now. Divorce is a sad but real fact of life in this day and age; shouldn't all women be prepared for this possibility? Isn't it just pragmatic to have a plan B in case one's relationship doesn't survive the ups and downs of life? Shouldn't all modern women give some thought to how we'll react or what we'll do when or if a divorce, breakup, or separation happens to us? Isn't it naïve to proceed without caution?

Some people would say yes. At one time I might have agreed also. But I'm here—after three hundred interviews with women in arranged marriages—to say no!

Regardless of how you justify, excuse, or deny it, partial commitment on any level negatively impacts your relationship or marriage by preventing you from being fully engaged in it. Instead, we undermine our marriage and our own potential happiness by consciously, subconsciously, or unconsciously subjecting the relationship to mental "reviews" or "assessments," particularly during difficult or trying times, with thoughts about whether we would be happier, better off, or more relaxed with someone else.

What About *His* Complete Commitment?

So, odds are that you might still have some problems with this point of view. "Sure, complete commitment sounds great, but doesn't it take *both* partners approaching the relationship like that for it to work? After all, what's the point of being completely committed if your partner isn't? If anything, doesn't that just make you more vulnerable?" Actually, no. Here's why.

Your complete commitment can lead to your partner's complete commitment.

I know it may sound like some sort of riddle, but here's how it works. When you relax into a mind-set of complete commitment, it changes how you respond to situations that previously would have been stressful or difficult or left you with feelings of insecurity. And since every action has a reaction, your partner's behavior will also change as he responds to the change in you.

Aleena had lived with James for five years before they broke up. Then she met and married Geoff, a classmate from business school. As she and Geoff began to approach their five-year anniversary, Aleena says she started to become increasingly convinced that this relationship would also soon be over. "I would go over all these different scenarios in my head, wondering how it would finally end, what he would say, and whether it would be like it was last time. I found myself starting to plan where I would live and how I would manage financially without his help." The result was that without Geoff having any idea what was going on, Aleena started to become increasingly distant and aloof from him, unconsciously pulling away as she prepared herself for a potential breakup.

Geoff had no idea what Aleena was worried about, but as she started to push him away and withdraw from the relationship, his behavior also started to change. "I fell in love with Geoff because he is so easygoing and relaxed, always making jokes and laughing," Aleena says. But as she became more worried, "he stopped being like that and things became really strained between us, which made me even more convinced that things were going to end."

Once the five-year mark passed, Aleena relaxed and things started to go back to how they were before. The change convinced her that if she was able to develop a mind-set of complete commitment, it could prevent anything like this from happening again.

Our societal fear of complete commitment, and the vulnerability associated with it, means that even when we may believe we are fully committed, too often on some level we keep the prospect of divorce or separation alive, and by doing so, we prevent ourselves and our partners from enjoying the benefits of total dedication to the relationship.

Fostering a sense of complete commitment can be difficult, but as Aleena agrees, "I really want to be together with Geoff forever, and I don't want to ruin it by being scared to really believe that it can happen." One way that Aleena—and all of us—can start to do this is to begin cultivating a more conscious awareness of the thought patterns and actions that either directly or indirectly lead to partial commitment.

It might sounds a little like New Age talk at first, but this issue relates to the oft-discussed law of attraction, made popular by the wildly successful 2006 bestseller, *The Secret*. In the words of one of the book's contributors, Michael Bernard Beckwith,

> What you are thinking about is creating your future life. You create your life with your thoughts. . . . What you think about the most or focus on the most is what will appear as your life. . . .
>
> If you are complaining, the law of attraction will powerfully bring into your life more situations for you to complain about. . . . The law is simply reflecting and giving back to you exactly what you are focusing on with your thoughts. With this powerful knowledge, you can completely change every circumstance and event in your entire life, by changing the way you think.

I believe this is entirely applicable to relationships. If you think about, focus on, and practice complete commitment, then that is what you will receive. And equally, if you focus on and prepare for problems, separation, or divorce, then that is what will come your way.

Exercise: Put It Down and Put It Away

If you are commitment-phobic and want to have a long-term relationship, you need to learn to put away the worries, anxieties, and negativity that you have around the idea of complete commitment.

How? You have to face your fears head-on.

1. First, decide what your relationship deal breakers are. For instance, physical abuse should always be one. So should extreme drug use, etc. Decide what is absolutely unforgivable for you. Remember, this is what is unforgivable for *you*; no one else's opinion matters. Write your personal deal breakers down on paper.

2. Next, let yourself think of all the situations that scare you—the what-ifs, small and large. Let your mind play out the complete scenarios. What would you really do if any of your fears actually happened? Write them down on paper or dictate them into a recorder, whatever feels better and more natural to you.

3. Then let all of your fears go. Say good-bye. Burn them. Flush them down the toilet. Roll them up and stick them in a bottle and drop the bottle in the ocean. Do whatever makes you feel rid of them forever!

When you face your fears and release them (this might be just the first step; you might want to do additional work with a life coach, therapist, or close friend), you can move forward with your life and your relationships, secure in the knowledge that if anything you wrote down happens, you'll trust yourself to know what to do. But you won't worry about it until then.

The Arranged-Marriage Way:
Decide to Commit. Period.

Couples in arranged marriages take the view that, barring certain extreme circumstances (such as severe addiction, serial adultery, abuse, or abandonment), divorce is just not an option. That's it. And so, with a mutual determined will to stay married, couples will do or try almost anything to stay together and make it work.

At first, this approach might sound highly rigid and limiting, but surprisingly, my interviews seemed to indicate that it actually has the opposite effect. Complete commitment allows both parties to feel fully secure in the relationship. When separation is not an option, traits or situations that might otherwise have been difficult or frustrating become much easier to handle. Even when the women I interviewed talked about a particularly difficult time in their marriages—from financial difficulties to family estrangement—they admitted that they rarely, if ever, even fleetingly considered separation or divorce as an option.

As Rebecca, a 44-year-old dentist from Pennsylvania, explained to me, "Why think about divorce? What's the point? I'm married and my husband's basically a good man. Yes, we have our problems; but tell me who doesn't? A new man just means a new and different set of problems." Rebecca can speak from experience. She has been married for over twenty years and she and her husband have gone through some tough periods. Severe family and business problems have left them barely talking for weeks at a time. But as she sternly told me, "The problem is that too many people think leaving is an answer to a problem. It's not; it just causes more of them."

It helps that the environment around arranged marriages, even those in North America, is strongly supportive of the idea of complete commitment. Extended family, friends, and community all come together to try and help couples work through their problems, insuring that the strength of their commitment is appreciated and reinforced.

When Sairika's husband, Kishan, started spending more and more evenings volunteering at a local charity, Sairika didn't even really notice. After almost twenty-five years of marriage, she felt comfortably safe with the way things were between them. But a few week later, at the supermarket, she noticed how he was acting with Paloma, the wife of a neighbor from their old neighborhood.

For the first time in their marriage, Sairika became suspicious. Suspicion turned to rage when she confronted Kishan about his behavior and he confessed that he and Paloma had been meeting for lunches and coffees for the past few week. He assured Sairika that they'd only been talking and that nothing else had happened, and he begged her forgiveness. Understandably, Sairika was hurt, angry, and confused.

Her teenage children, hearing their parents' arguments, also stepped in. The situation was now dividing the family. As she remembers, "I genuinely didn't know what to do, whether they'd been talking or if something more had happened. A part of me didn't even care since either way he'd lied to me, dishonored our marriage, and made a fool of me in front of my family and community. I couldn't imagine leaving. But I also couldn't imagine how I could still have him around." Their daughter Sybil, now 23 and drifting in and out of the room while I was speaking with her mother in their comfortable family room, joined in at one point. "It was like Mom and Dad were at a breaking point then. I was scared, since I really thought they could go either way."

What brought Sairika and Kishan back together was the complete conviction of their community of friends, family, and temple congregation that they would work through this issue.

Everyone rallied around and worked to remind the couple both individually and together of how important what they shared was, all that they had built for their family, and why and how it was so necessary that they work through this now. "People shared their own stories about difficult times they had had. I know that Kishan's brothers and cousins both talked to him. Their belief that this was a small thing in the course of our years together was what sustained me and brought us back together.

"It wasn't easy at all, I was angry almost every day. Looking back at those months, it was the sheer belief that everyone around us had that Kishan and I would not only get through this, but that it would be a small piece in our bigger story that played a really large role in our ability to discuss why this happened and figure out the steps to make sure it never happened again."

Is Adultery Really So Rampant?

In our sex-obsessed culture, one of the first thoughts that probably comes to mind when you hear the words "complete commitment" is that it means "no sex outside of marriage or the relationship." And while that's true (since obviously adultery is a severe blow to the foundations of any relationship), you don't even have to be having sex with someone else to be undermining your relationship.

Emotional infidelity—whether it's flirty e-mails to your sexy colleague, long phone conversations to your old boyfriend from college, or just emotionally and mentally removing yourself from the relationship by thinking of options without your partner or spouse—can all have an equally detrimental effect on a relationship.

While we tend to overlook the risks and dangers of the above, many women say that while complete commitment may sound great, if a man cheated she'd be out the door in a heart-beat. Well, that may be true, and of course I understand it. But, just take a moment to consider this: "If he cheats, I'm outta here" feeling may be another component of the partial commitment, the one foot out the door sydrome.

In fact, an April 2007 MSNBC.com/iVillage survey shows that most Americans fear adultery more than they need to, probably because images of and news about infidelity are everywhere in popular culture. The article described how more than seventy thousand adults completed this survey online, and iVillage found that survey takers guessed that *twice* as many people were having extramarital affairs than actually are. Yes, some people cheat, but not nearly as many as we fear.

The arranged marriage approach of complete commitment works because, contrary to how it might appear at first, this level of determined commitment to a relationship is actually highly liberating.

What arranged marriages show is that when you take away the option of separation or divorce (except in the most exceptional of circumstances), it actually makes it easier for couples to address and overcome various divisions or problems. The way it works is that when this level of commitment exists, both people can feel secure in the strength of the commitment and relax into the relationship, knowing that with the exception of a few clearly defined and very serious issues, they will stay with their partner. End of story. On a day-to-day basis (which is really where so many relationships are won or lost), this means they are less likely to worry about the small issues, whether they can do better, and just generally about the future of their relationship. Wouldn't that be a nice feeling!

Anu is 38-year-old PA in Long Island who says that she sort of "fell into" an arranged marriage. "I was interested in something serious and my parents were pushing me to at least see people." (Note: This is arranged-marriage code for starting the screening and introduction process.) "I said I would keep dating, but that I didn't mind meeting people that they found, if the guys met what I was looking for."

She laughingly admits that the first two meetings "were disasters! I was convinced that I'd made a huge mistake just by agreeing to humor my parents." But as the cliché goes, the third time was the charm. Anu and Kirin met in the living room of her parents' house in Buffalo, where his parents lived also. Kirin, a 39-year-old graphic designer, appealed to Anu as soon as they met. "Kirin just seemed so relaxed about what was really a pretty nerve-wracking situation. He told me that at first he'd agreed to meet people to make his elderly parents happy, but that after a couple of meetings, he found that he really liked a lot of the women he was meeting, but so far it just hadn't come together." But it did for them. They exchanged e-mails for a couple of weeks and met again (with both their parents present). At that meeting, three weeks after their first meeting, they got engaged.

Now married four years, Anu says this is the first time that she feels able to say what she really means and feels, even if she knows it will lead to a fight. "Growing up, I looked different than everyone else and never felt attractive. Once I started dating, I always had a real sense of trying not to stir things up since I was so scared that the guy would leave. Kirin and I definitely fight, or as I like to call it, 'vigorously disagree,' but it doesn't scare me the way it used to before, since I know neither of us is going anywhere."

Arranged marriages are premised on a level of commitment that frees the relationship from the moods, disagreements, or stresses of different life stages. This means that couples are able to disagree and robustly argue a topic without the underlying threat that these differences will threaten the foundation of the relationship.

Similarly, when you are completely committed, it naturally becomes easier to focus on the positives of the relationship instead of the problems. Although I am not in an arranged marriage, this is something I noticed when I first got married. There was something about the level of commitment that my husband Rana and I now had that made me overlook small habits of his that might have irritated me in the past or—let's be honest—even have led me to reconsider the whole relationship! Suddenly it just seemed silly and pointless to dwell on these thoughts, since I wasn't going to take any action around them and it wasn't doing me any good to feel annoyed. As a result, I just ignored the small stuff (and still do!) and went on with the business of my life. And along the way, I realized that most of these "annoying" things were so small or insignificant, compared with being married and having a family together, that I've gradually stopped even noticing them.

The arranged-marriage level of commitment frees couples from the what-if thoughts that undermine a relationship. Instead, they are able to enjoy an absolute commitment that infuses the couple with a sense of deep security that so many of us—with our checkered pasts, cautious walls, and fearfulness—are never able to enjoy.

One of my favorite interviews was with 57-year-old Arti, a lively woman with a ready laugh who instantly makes you feel like you've known her for years and hope you'll know her for many more. Arti had an arranged marriage "a lifetime ago!" when she was 19 and still living with her parents in Kenya. She met her husband once in a roomful of people that included both their extended families. "In our community, and at that time in East Africa, it was considered quite progressive to let the bride and groom meet like that, with everyone watching. We were both so nervous, though, I remember us just mumbling a few lines at each other's shoes. I never even looked up at his face and then had to keep asking my cousins and aunts for descriptions of him!" Two months after they were married, they moved to Canada, where Arti's new husband had gotten a job.

"At that time in Canada and where we lived, Indians were rare, and so the women I met kept asking me questions about my marriage. I didn't mind; it helped me find out about how things worked over here." Taking another sip of her coffee, she continues. "They were always surprised when I told them that Nitin and I had had a fight the night before or that I'd yelled at him about something. I guess they thought that since I'd had an arranged marriage, I would never actually speak my mind to my husband! This made me laugh, since I'd grown up in a house where no matter how sweet my mother might have seemed on the surface, she ruled the family, including my father, when it came to anything to do with money, family decisions, or business.

"After all these years together, Nitin and I know each other so well, what's there left to fight about? But in the beginning, I was never shy to tell him what I felt or thought. I had a real sense that we were partners, building a life and trying to establish ourselves. We were in this together and he needed to know what I thought.

"It's funny," she muses, "I really don't see that level of confidence in my daughter's marriage." I know Arti's daughter, Maya, from college, which is how I came to be sitting here interviewing Arti. Maya had been engaged to a student from her class in medical school, but after a year, he broke it off. A couple of years ago she married a French academic and moved to the UK. "Even though they've been married for two and a half years and recently had a daughter, Maya is still so hesitant and tentative with her husband. It worries me. It wasn't how she used to be, but after her former fiancé left like that, it really shattered her confidence and faith in relationships."

The way Maya seems to lack confidence in the durability of her marriage is quite common among women who've spent years of our lives dating. After the first time someone leaves or lets us down, it becomes increasingly difficult to jump back into a relationship with the same level of trust, faith, and commitment. And no matter how much it may ultimately hurt the current relationship, it becomes difficult to expose yourself again.

It's a theme I heard echoed in several conversations during my interviews, among them with Ruby, the art dealer discussed in Chapter 2 who had decided to have an arranged marriage after realizing she was constantly dating men she couldn't relax with. "I used to hold myself back in past relationships. A classic case of being scared of giving too much or falling too deeply, I would instead always be censoring myself to try and fit in to what I thought the man of the moment wanted for me. That changed when I married Sanjay. Since I've never felt safer or more accepted, it's given me a different level of confidence to just be myself."

Want more proof of the power and happiness potential of complete commitment? A survey published in the June 1996 issue of *Social Psychology Quarterly* reported that couples (in nonarranged marriages) who make it to their thirty-fifth anniversary actually find themselves happier with each other than they were as newlyweds.

My interview with Kriya particularly stands out to me. Kriya was 85 when we spoke. Still elegant in her navy and silver sari with matching jewelry, she and her husband live between their house in Delhi and the homes of their fifteen grandchildren. She married at 16 and is from a very traditional family; even after an amazing seventy years together, she still doesn't call her husband by name when talking about him or to him! (Believe it or not, there's an even more formal practice out there. My great-grandmother followed the tradition of dropping the first letter of her husband's name from any word that started with that letter. So, if his name was Paul, she would pronounce the word "pill" as "ill" or "parent" as "aren't." Seriously confusing stuff!)

Over the course of several conversations, Kriya told me about her life with her husband, and how they essentially grew up together. Over their many decades together, the couple raised their family, rescued his family's failing import-export business, saw their parents get sick and die, endured the death of a sibling each, and shared everything else that life brought their way. When I asked Kriya what she thought of the study I just mentioned, she laughed and said that seemed early in the relationship! But she admitted that, yes, once the kids were settled and married, she and her husband did enjoy being together more. "It was as if we had our childhoods back, but were together, with no parents to worry about, no children, no working and worrying all the time. We had more fun. We both learned about baseball and started going to games when we went to visit our grandchildren."

When I asked her what it was like after almost seventy years together, she simply said, "Ab to hum ek hi jaan hain," which essentially translates to, "We are like one now." I don't know about you, but I'll take Kriya's definition of one above our false notion of "the one" any day!

What This Means for You

All right, it's really romantic and sweet to talk about couples who've been married for fifty, sixty, seventy years, but how is that relevant or helpful to a single woman wanting to get married right now?

Well, here it is: if you're in a relationship, whether it's brand-new or a few years into it, then actively and daily start practicing the thought and speech patterns around complete commitment. This is key to your taking the relationship to the next level and fighting the impact that our environment of partial commitment will have on you unless you consciously guard against it. This means actively being conscious and aware of the words and thoughts you use that subconsciously undermine the idea of complete commitment.

A hint: do whatever it takes. This change in your thinking is crucial to your long-term happiness. I'm reminded of my friend Carla, who has a habit of wearing a hair band around her wrist as a reminder to herself to do different things—from stopping herself from eating junk food when she's on a diet to remembering to indulge in only two drinks at work events. Anyway, Carla's new thing is that she uses the hair band (and the occasional—and painful—snap of it against her wrist) to remind herself to pay attention to the positive aspects of her eleven-month relationship with her new boyfriend, Brandon.

Her report-back after two weeks of the hair band trick: "I love Brandon. I mean, this is the first guy I've met that I really think about having children and doing that whole bit with. So I was completely shocked with how often I found myself still having thoughts or saying things to him or my mom that were all against the idea that we would actually work out. It's like, without realizing it, I was setting myself up for this not to work out, just like my past relationships!"

Okay, so the hair band is a good trick (although admittedly a little strange!) for those of you in a current relationship. What if you're dating, in a dry spell, or still waiting to meet a man who makes you even want complete commitment? In that case—same advice!

You should still watch your thoughts, your patterns, and your relationship expectations so you notice how it all affects the way in which you have internalized the environment of partial commitment. This doesn't mean committing to the next man you go for a drink with or suddenly planning a life with your single colleague. It *does* mean letting go of your baggage around complete commitment and changing the way you let the environment of partial commitment affect you. It means no more cynical comments or bitter little quips about men being scared of commitment! It means no more moaning that there are no good men out there. It means no more jokey little remarks like telling your friends that you love tapas because you can't even commit to a dinner entrée. You can start feeling positive about commitment today. Right now. It's simply a shift in your mind.

After her first marriage failed, Barb, 32, stepped back into the dating world for the first time in eight years. "Maybe I did it too soon, but I was so angry and jaded about the way things had failed with Peter that I became one of those women who always had a joke about men being dogs or marriage being a waste of time and it all being pointless. I didn't realize how I appeared or sounded until a man I had grown up with told me that I was starting to frighten him with my negativity."

If you're not in a relationship right now, this change in thinking is extremely important. You need to start believing that complete commitment is a positive thing that will free you and allow you to experience a greater level of relationship happiness and fulfillment than before. If you start now, you'll be commitment-ready by the time you meet that fabulous, commitment-ready man you've been looking for!

Living This Secret

- **Beware "one foot out the door" and "something better" syndromes.** This type of thinking may feel practical, but it's extremely damaging to a relationship. If you keep your options open and keep looking for a better situation, you're likely to end up alone and empty-handed.

- **Hang out with people who want you to be happy.** Just as you wouldn't hang out with heavy drinkers if you're trying to stay sober, don't hang out with relationship bashers if you're trying to find a committed relationship. Hanging out with negative people will lead you to make negative comments and feel negative. Either stop chatting with such people about dating or spend your time with happy couples and optimistic daters.

- **Watch your words.** Sticks and stones might break your bones . . . and words can be even more damaging. So start paying attention to the words you use when it comes to your current partner or relationships and commitment in general. It doesn't matter if you're talking to your mom, your best friend, your new boyfriend, or yourself—stop it now!

Chapter Four

It Doesn't Matter
If He Doesn't Dance

The Danger of Confusing
Common Interests with Shared Values

Best friends Kelly and Deena were both going through a dating dry spell. "It felt like it had been months since either of us had met anyone with any sort of dating or relationship potential," says Deena, the 32-year-old owner of a small dog-grooming business. "I don't tend to meet many guys at my job and Kelly works for herself from home, so she meets even fewer than I do!" They'd both talked about trying online dating, but each was reluctant to take the first step and actually do it. "I just know that I would never feel comfortable describing myself to people I'd never met. Even in small groups I hate talking about myself," Kelly admits.

One Sunday over brunch, the two of them thought that they had found the solution—one of those dating websites that would let them post profiles not for themselves but for each other. Each friend would screen possibilities for the other one. "I was really excited," Kelly admits. "I mean, I've known Deena since we were ten and we started going to the same camp every summer. I would say that she knows me better than anyone." Deena agreed. "Kelly knows all my likes, dislikes, hobbies, the whole package. I figured if anyone could find me my Mr. Right, it would be Kelly."

And so each took the other person's picture, filled out her profile, and went through the possible candidates to decide on a date. "Part of our deal was that we couldn't tell the other person anything about who she was going to meet and that we both had to go on the date on the same night."

Deena loves animals and is very athletic, so Kelly set her up with someone who listed sports as his favorite pastime and had a profile picture of himself with his dog. When the big night came, they met at a bar that he suggested. "I can't believe Kelly didn't pick up on the fact that a man who suggests a first date at a loud sports bar with peanuts and popcorn on the floor is, um, probably *not* my type!"

The date didn't start well, and the way Deena describes it, it pretty much went downhill from there. "Saying that sports were a 'hobby' for this guy was a vast understatement. It was the only thing he could talk about. I think he'd been some big college athlete and just couldn't get over it. He didn't ask me one thing about myself or my business. I don't know what Kelly was thinking. I had nothing in common with this guy!"

It was hard for Deena to be too irritated about it though, since her choice for Kelly was hardly much better. Kelly is a freelance writer and jewelry designer who loves old musicals and vintage clothes. She's also a great skier. Keeping these interests in mind, Deena set her up with a man named Alex, who listed skiing, dancing, theater, and musicals in his profile. Sounds perfect, right? "He was okay, I guess," Kelly reflects, "but he had been married twice and had three kids, and I was just really unimpressed with the way he spoke about them. Afterward, Deena kept going on about how not that many men were probably interested in musicals. I don't know why she was so focused on that one thing, though! Who cares if he likes them? Deena's my best friend and she hates them, so it's hardly a deal breaker for me."

Deena's focus on finding someone for Kelly who was also interested in musicals and Kelly's comment that she didn't know why it mattered so much, highlight one of the most damaging and misleading approaches to dating and relationships.

Unfortunately, it's also among the most common.

The Hobby Hoax

The principle seems to make sense: find someone with whom you share interests or hobbies and you'll be happy together. It's also one of the tritest pieces of relationship and dating advice out there. Each month magazines are filled with articles on how and why women should join a class or take up a hobby to help them meet a man who's right for them. Or if they are already in a relationship, they should get their partner to sign up for dance lessons or Italian cooking classes together, as a way to become closer. This advice appears to be smart and harmless. After all, wouldn't having an interest in common give a couple something to build a relationship around?

It certainly can't hurt a relationship, but shared interests are not really that important. After all, how strong or desirable is a relationship built around the fact that you both like bird-watching or scrapbooking? As we'll see in this chapter, arranged marriages show us that the classic advice of seeking a man with common interests actually gets in the way of finding a lifelong mate. Turns out that ignoring this advice will actually give you a far better chance of meeting the kind of husband-worthy man you are looking for.

What you need is to find someone who shares your life and relationship *values*—it's back to your marriage musts again. Despite what you may think right now, nothing else—from music tastes to whether or not he can ski or has an interest in walking around art exhibits—means a thing when it comes to finding a lifelong partner.

Many women get concerned about the lack of common interests with their boyfriends. But shouldn't the focus be whether he shares your *life* passions? Your passion for family, honesty, spirituality, kindness, justice, or whatever your most deeply held beliefs are? I know I've said it earlier in the book, but it's so important that it's worth repeating: your marriage musts are all that matter. Kristin, a 34-year-old concert violinist, found out (twice!) that even a shared devotion to one's life's work isn't enough to make a relationship work.

Music is literally a way of life for Kristin. She's toured the world with a number of different orchestras and spends hours each day practicing. She says that her music has "essentially consumed my life for the past twenty years, ever since my first audition for a special music high school when I was fourteen." Since music was so much more than just a hobby, "I always thought that I would only be able to love someone who shared the same sort of all-consuming commitment that I have."

As a result, both of her last two boyfriends were also classical musicians. "Both times I went into the relationship with such high hopes, thinking that with our shared love of music, our common schedules, our passion for this art, we would be soul mates. I was so convinced of this that I overlooked everything else about both of them."

Sadly, neither relationship turned out the way Kristin hoped. "The only thing worse than the year I spent with Steven were the two years that I wasted on Glenn." Kristin's dream of a shared passion bringing her relationship closer disintegrated amid increasingly acrimonious fights with both men. "I can't just blame them. I mean, they brought out a competitive and vicious streak in me that matched theirs."

She sighs. "My best friend is an opera singer and when she married a lawyer who knew nothing about her art, I thought she was crazy and told her so at the time. I just couldn't get beyond the idea that he wasn't a musician and didn't care about opera. Well, clearly she knew more than I did, since they've been married for almost six years now and I have never seen a happier or more balanced couple."

It wasn't music that tore apart her last two relationships; it's that Kristin didn't pay attention to anything beyond their common talent and career choice. Regardless of how much each man may have shared her passion, it wasn't enough to save a relationship when no one had even *considered* their marriage musts!

Since very few of us are actually so defined by one specific trait or vocation, Kristin may seem like a bit of a special example. But the reason I chose to share her story is that it so clearly illustrates how this thinking works. Yes, Glenn and Steven both shared her passion for music, but based on that, Kristin simply assumed that they would also share the other values that have led to her build her life around her art. And while I was talking to her, it struck me that part of the problem was also the incredibly high expectations that she had for both relationships. It was clear that Kristin had associated the shared passion for music with the belief that this would create a greater bond to their relationship. This could have been possible (as we will see in Chapter 7), but it works only if the fundamental groundwork—those marriage musts—are already in place. Again, we come back to the damaging effects of so many women's belief in the idea of a soul mate—that one person on the planet who's "the one." And the fantasy around the idea of a soul mate is that Mr. Right will share all your interests and the two of you will spend most of your time blissfully sequestered together and focused on each other.

This brings us back to the issue of being responsible for your own happiness. The more content and secure you are with your own hobbies, talents, and interests, the less important it is to find a partner who shares the exact same ones. Come to think of it, that might take away from your individuality and self-esteem.

While I have a tendency to blame every unrealistic relationship expectation on the media (apologies to all of you readers who work for magazines, TV shows, and advertising agencies!), in this case I think we ourselves have to take some of the blame. In some ways, the desire to find a mate based simply on shared interests is a cop-out. It's not always easy to do the personal reflection needed to try and live a life based on values. And that's why it's not easy to determine one's marriage musts. Often, in the chaos and frenzy of life, our focus is so much on the day-to-day, just getting by and getting through, that we rarely have the chance or the inclination to figure out *what* our actual life and relationship values really are (just one more reminder to go back and do your marriage musts list in Chapter 2 if you haven't already).

As a result, we often don't know what we are really looking for in a relationship since we don't know who we are. And in this absence or void, similar to the way in which so many people take their identity from their careers, we take the more superficial aspects of our lives or personalities and mistake them for our relationship values or marriage musts.

When we don't know what we're looking for to feed our deepest wants and needs, we risk overvaluing what are often passing or surface interests—like hobbies, sports teams, types of food, or particular musicians.

That's what happened with 34-year-old Heather and her last boyfriend. "Sam and I got together when we were both twenty-six and just finishing up our graduate degrees. Sam was—well, I guess he still is—totally about saving the world, everything was a cause. In fact, one of his favorite sayings was that every action is political. Whether we were buying groceries or just getting a coffee, we had to analyze the message. I admired it; after all, I had been part of all the same activist groups on campus. I couldn't wait to get married to him at the time."

So if they shared so much, what happened? Well, it turns out, for Heather, much of her interest in these causes had more to do with the people she had initially met. For her it was more social than deeply meaningful. "To be honest, I got into a lot of these causes because my roommate was always inviting me to meetings. Once I met Sam, I kept going, and soon I thought that was really me. But as I got older and left college, I realized that, unlike Sam, I didn't want my whole life to be a political struggle. It was like I suddenly realized that as much as I'm interested in all the things that Sam is, I don't actually want that every single day. I want something and someone different. Now when I go out and start dating again, I want to be really careful that I don't let myself get confused by what I might be slightly interested in versus what I actually want to be important in my real life." Of course I told Heather that the best way to do this is to get clear on her marriage musts!

I think one of the best ways to prove just how misleading our belief in the importance of common interests or hobbies are is to pick up the Personals section of your local paper or check out the ads on a dating website. How many people really list their marriage musts? It seems to feel safer or easier to list interests you'd like to share with a partner, such as tennis, theater, or going to the beach.

I know that it might feel weird to list "desire for a family, deep honesty, support for a strong woman, and empathy for those in need" on Match.com or in a public newspaper. So I recommend that you think about activities and interests that reflect or embody your marriage musts. Even if you never actually write a personal ad, practice writing a dating profile here that would really reflect what you want in a life partner.

When I tried this, I carefully selected hobbies or interests that I thought would be illustrative of marriage musts for me. For instance, I listed bikram (or hot) yoga as one of my interests. This wasn't because I necessarily wanted to date someone who also practices that form of yoga, but because I wanted someone committed to working out and spirituality. Another friend tells me she was attracted to her current fiancé because he listed in his dating profile that he subscribed to *The Economist* and *The New Yorker*. To her, these were signs that he was intellectually curious and concerned about the larger world—both important values and marriage musts to her.

So, in your journal or on a piece of paper, take a shot at writing a dating profile that is based on your marriage musts. Include interests or activities that reflect your most important values. Only list things that would attract a man who meets your marriage musts. Making the distinction between your deepest life values and the interests you enjoy pursuing is a crucial step in the process of attracting a lifelong mate. When difficult situations arise in life (as they inevitably do), you won't care if your husband is a good doubles partner or knows his jazz musicians. You'll want to know that he is there for you in every way you need.

"He's Not My Type" Revisited: The Trap of the Type

In the world of clichéd breakup lines, right up there with "I meant to call" and "It's me and not you" has to be the all-purpose and all-encompassing explanation, "He just wasn't my type."

This can mean anything and everything, from the serious (he

didn't meet your marriage musts) to the superficial (he doesn't go to the same clubs as you do, you didn't like his outfit, or, as one friend recently told me about her last date, "We just wouldn't look right next to each other"). Just like the hobby hoax, the type trap is the belief that, based on superficial, transient, and change-able characteristics, a person can identify his or her "type"—the one kind of person who will be a good match. This belief is so ingrained in us that if we think of ourselves as the Boho, free-spirit type, it may never occur to us even to think about dating from the nerdy IT or jock category. If this is starting to feel like high school, well, that's a clue as to how immature this thought pattern can be.

As I discussed in Chapter 2, when it comes to dating, we limit ourselves with the type trap, and by doing so, we restrict our op-tions and potentially overlook prospects that meet all our core marriage musts but just may not immediately "look" or "feel" the part.

What would you say your type is? Why? What is it based on? How has it changed over the years? Now reverse the questions! Whose type are you? And what do you think *that* is based on? Do you feel that the type that others might ascribe to you accurately reflects who you are, what you are about, or what you bring to a relationship? And might that change over a lifetime?

When you turn the conversation around and think about what type you yourself are, you start to realize how superficial the whole concept is. Typecasting causes us to dismiss or pre-judge people without even seeing if they meet our marriage musts. Would you want someone to dismiss you because of what sports you like, what movies you enjoy, or what table you sat at in the high school cafeteria (or whether you were the kid outside smoking instead of eating lunch)? I certainly wouldn't.

This is what Gail found out when the sheer persistence of her cousin Anthony resulted in her starting to date a man who

Gail laughingly admits was the epitome of "not her type." She says, "Ten years ago when I was a teenager, you couldn't have paid me to go on a date with someone like Phil. But these ten months that we've been together have been some of the best I've ever had."

Gail has had what she happily calls a "hodgepodge" career; she plays in a band, does some freelance sound editing, teaches an art class for kids, and attempts "whatever else comes my way that sounds like fun." Her look is also a bit of a hodgepodge: she has long dark hair with platinum (and one fluorescent pink) streaks, and on the day we met, she was wearing a soft pink baby-doll dress, with black lace-up boots, leggings, and what looked like a poncho. "I'm telling you; the only reason Phil and I got together is that my cousin Anthony literally just kept bringing us together. I have no idea what he possibly saw in the two of us that made him think that we would work together!"

On the surface, it's hard not to agree with her. Phil is an IT journalist; he writes for a trade publication that covers things like developments in the data storage sector, which he absolutely loves. In contrast to Heather's eclectic style, his look is more suburban dad on a day off—jeans that are a little too tight, too short, and sitting at his waist, topped off by T-shirts and plastic windbreakers with logos of database and enterprise companies on them. "It wasn't until our third meeting, when we all went for drinks and I ended up sitting next to Phil, that I realized how much fun he was. And even more, that our approach to life, career, and family was so surprisingly in tune."

Bingo! Gail discovered that when she met a man who shared her marriage musts, not much else mattered, particularly not what "type" he was, or what she would have thought of such a guy in high school. I mean, think about it: what could be worse than to be dating in your twenties and thirties based on who you liked or how you saw yourself when you were 17!

I do admit that if you are accustomed to looking for a certain set of characteristics in a mate, it can be difficult to break out of that familiar pattern. That's what 36-year-old Susan, whom I would describe as a New York fashionista, found when she tried to break her pattern of the past fifteen years of dating trendy hipster types. Susan writes for a website that reviews the latest and most exclusive hotels, restaurants, and spas. The job really suits her, since she is someone who seems to effortlessly pull off the latest runway look and constantly receives invitations to the most glamorous private parties.

Since Susan first moved from college in New Hampshire to the city, she's been dating a string of men who most definitely looked like her type—you know, the sort of man who can actually pull off three-quarter-length Capri pants and open-to-the-chest linen shirts. "I know I have a type, and for the past twelve years, I've pretty much kept to it," she says. "It's partly because that's who I was meeting, but also because I suppose that's who I saw myself with. I just couldn't picture how someone who didn't fit this mold would be attractive to me."

But as Susan admits, her last few years of dating in this scene have "left me feeling really lonely. I mean, I really feel like the last few years have been about dating men where the main things we have in common are a shared love of Italian designers and the ability to get reservations at the hot new sushi restaurant. It's the kind of thing that I was excited about in my twenties and it was still pretty exciting in my early thirties, but I'm done. I need to move on to something more fulfilling, and soon!"

Despite saying it, Susan admits that this has been harder than she thought. "Well, I want to meet someone who shares more of the values I grew up with. I'm not saying that it couldn't happen with the guys I know, but it hasn't yet. I want to try dating some other types of men, but then I just think, What would a guy who thinks fleece is okay in the evening ever have in common with me?"

And so, a year after we first had this conversation, Sarah remains stuck in this frustrating and lonely cycle. I can't help but wonder if whether or not he wears fleece is really that important.

The Arranged-Marriage Way:
Values Are Front and Center

In an arranged marriage, while the parents or some other close senior family member generally manages the selection and screening process, the person looking for a match usually has quite a bit of input in terms of the criteria for possible candidates. He or she can be very honest about what values are important. There is no need to hide one's values to make a dating profile seem less revealing. Men and women seeking arranged marriages are encouraged to openly select criteria that relate to their desire for a happy marriage and secure future.

Noticeably and consistently absent from the marriage musts lists of the women I interviewed was any mention of hobbies or interests. This struck me, particularly after I recently set up a friend on a dinner date based on the fact that she and the guy both loved golf and had lived in France. Knowing what I do now, it's no big surprise that it didn't work out. The next day I interviewed a woman in an arranged marriage who told me that she had agreed to marry her husband with absolutely zero knowledge about what her husband liked to do in his free time—whether he was a reader, a soap opera fanatic, or a salsa dancer. It just didn't matter to her because his values and life plans were exactly in line with hers.

At the time, I remember thinking that at least *some* attention should be paid to common interests in an arranged marriage, just so the couple has something to talk about when they're alone together the first time! I made a note to bring it up at my next interview, and when I did, the woman I was interviewing—the mother of a close friend—just started laughing.

"No one thought about hobbies or things like that when they were arranging a marriage. Marriage is an important decision, and things like that aren't important to marriage! At the most, maybe they would mention that someone is good at music, but that's just a sort of side conversation thing."

This was a new concept for me, but one that, as my interviews progressed, became increasingly clear. Arranged marriages are about values, and a practical approach to life and marriage. Things like hobbies and interests would just never be given any weight. Once I had noticed this phenomenon, I realized that all these years I had been overlooking the most obvious example of all: my own parents!

Probably like many of you, my views on my parents' thirty-five-year marriage have shifted based on my own life experience. The older I get, the more I realize that they actually have a fairly vibrant, strong marriage. Interestingly, though, I can't really think of anything specific that they do together or hobbies that they share. My father is a fanatic bridge player. He plays tournaments at local clubs, socially and online. My mother never plays cards and, despite years of my father's trying to get her interested, she's remained constant on this one. My mother reads widely—everything from political books to literature to detective mysteries. She follows fashion and old movies and has a wide circle of friends. The two of them take regular walks together, but that's about it. And yet, I think their marriage has actually benefited from this. Each is interested in different things, and brings something new to the marriage conversation as a result.

What I found particularly interesting during my interviews was how women who had previously dated and had grown up in the United States found the transition of attention away from a type during the arranged-marriage process.

"I've never really known what my type was! Maybe that's why I was never very good at dating," Sheena, my eyebrow waxer tells me during one of my multitasking appointments. "I never thought I would have an arranged marriage. I mean, when I was young I just thought they were so weird! What changed it for me is that I really liked both my brother-in-law and my cousin's husband so much, and those were arranged marriages. I still don't know what my type is, but I'm happy with my husband, so I guess it no longer really matters."

Interests, hobbies, types—as we've seen, none of these things figure into the arranged-marriage equation very much at all. And if anything, they are bonuses or afterthoughts. Women in arranged marriages don't have to worry about missing out on men who don't seem like whatever they perceive to be their type. In fact, the process is specifically designed to prevent that. Couples are brought together on the basis of their shared values and characteristics, such as education, family, and culture. The arranged-marriage view is that these are what create the foundation for a stable and rewarding relationship over the long term and throughout various life stages. The arranged-marriage view or approach is that since the couple has this common foundation, the act of building a life and family together will be more than enough to get them started.

As Priya, a human resources consultant in Boston, told me, "I wouldn't say that my husband and I like to do many of the same things together. Things like that I have more in common with my friends. But then I'm not living with them, raising three girls, and building my future with my friends. I'm doing that with Prakash, so I find it doesn't actually matter what our hobbies are since we already share all the important things, which is enough."

This approach works because, freed as they are from the beliefs and myths about what a happy relationship or a "couple in love" does, women in arranged marriages genuinely don't seem to think that shared interest are all that important. Instead, they focus on what they do have together, which are the more meaningful things, such as family, future plans, and ethical beliefs. By focusing on sharing these things, they shift their attention to the positive, rather than dwelling on whatever the couple doesn't have in common.

Again, since women in arranged marriages don't have the burden of media and cultural pressure about finding the one who shares their every interest, they are free from that cultural baggage. They don't worry that a lack of shared hobbies must mean that they aren't meant to be together with their husbands. And if you're looking for a life partner, you shouldn't worry about that either.

What This Means for You

Both the hobby hoax and the type trap are common relationship red herrings—things that don't actually matter when it comes to successful dating and happy long-term relationships, but things that we have falsely believed to be important. The idea that you need to have hobbies or interests in common with a possible partner or date is completely misleading. Letting go of this belief allows you to really think about the values and traits that you want from a partner. There is truth in the saying, Don't sweat the small stuff. Unlike the majority of relationship books and magazine articles out there, talk show host and bestselling author Dr. Phil is one of the few who advises that's it's a myth that a great relationship requires common interests to bind you together. Instead, he advises that it doesn't help the relationship when you push your partner into unnatural interests.

So let go of these old ideas. Instead, I invite you to resolve right now to actively expand your dating pool and options! Make a list of three "types" that you would never have previously considered and open yourself up to the possibility that a guy you never would have dated in the past could be a great match. You don't even have to go on a date with such a person—just open your mind to the possibility. Then, the next time you meet any guy who doesn't immediately appear to be a match, hopefully, you'll be more open to checking him out a bit more, looking deeper, and not making a snap judgment about him. Any guy— short, towering, skinny, heavy, hairy, lithe, blue-eyed, big-nosed, bald, mop-headed, leather-wearing, preppy, whatever!—could meet your marriage musts. But you won't know until you look beneath the surface stuff.

Dating and relationships are hard enough, so don't complicate them even further! Expand your options and you'll expand your chances of success. Don't limit yourself to the false belief that you have a type. In fact, the belief that you have a type limits you to a pretty boring life. Think of all the new experiences, interests, and lessons you'll miss if you marry someone who is only interested in the same stuff you are.

Another bonus of ditching the belief in a type is that you will stop worrying about changing any guy you meet. If you accept that different interests are a good thing and that whether you share them is actually no reflection on the strength or potential of your relationship, you'll stop feeling like you need to make him the perfect guy who is your male twin. No more feeling the pressure to change him, change yourself, or change together to meet someone else's ideas of what a happy couple looks like and does together! Let your guy sit there alphabetizing his video game collection while you go out for a run. Let him weed in the garden while you strum on your guitar in the garage. Vive la difference! As long as a man meets your marriage musts, stop worrying about types and enjoy living your lives side by side.

Living This Secret

- **Defy the hobby hoax.** Having shared interests or hobbies doesn't matter when it comes to long-term marital happiness. Shared values are infinitely more important and a better indicator of compatibility over a lifetime.

- **Don't fall into the type trap.** The marriage musts are the foundation of a good relationship. Everything else is just window dressing. After all, would you want a man to choose you as a life partner because of what you wear or what clique you hung out with in high school?

- **Vive la difference!** You don't need to do everything with your partner; it's actually a positive thing to have your own interests. You'll also take the pressure off your relationship when you accept each other for exactly who you are and what you like to do, whether together or alone.

Chapter Five

Secret #5

Romance Needs a Rewrite

Ditch Valentine's Day and Instead
Decide What's Really Important to You

~~Casablanca~~
~~The Bridges of Madison County~~
~~Sleeping Beauty~~
~~Every Meg Ryan movie ever made~~

Christy describes herself as a romantic, a real girl's girl. She's always loved makeup, dressing up, and, of course, chick flicks. As a little girl, her favorites were *Cinderella* and *Snow White*. As she got older, her faves shifted to *Father of the Bride* and *Legally Blonde*. She laughingly admits that she's seen *Sweet Home Alabama* at least ten times and that her favorite part is the engagement scene when Reese Witherspoon's fiancé takes her to Tiffany's in New York. In this scene, he's arranged to have the store opened at night so she can wander through the glass cases and have her pick of the sparkling diamond engagement rings.

Christy has been in a steady long-term relationship with

George, an engineer, for the past two and a half years. They're planning to get engaged in the next year or so.

"I've always thought that a woman's engagement is one of the most important days of her life," Christy tells me. "It sounds so horrible, but I feel that with George, I just know it won't be anything romantic or special, and that instead there's a good chance I'll be starting my married life already disappointed. To be honest, I'm just dreading the way George will probably propose when he gets around to it. Knowing him, it could be over a DVD and an order of Chinese takeout one Friday night when I'm looking terrible in my sweats and we're just crashed out on the couch."

Even a quick chat with George gives you the sense that, as Christy describes, he's probably not the sort of man to go in for extravagant gestures. Just from a brief meeting, he looked to me like he's more the quiet, steady, solid type. And it turns out he is. For instance, he's waiting until he's helped Christy pay off her substantial student and personal loans before he proposes. Christy also mentions that he regularly goes over to her divorced mother's house to help her with any repairs or maintenance that needs to be done.

While Christy appreciates that side of him, she also dismisses it, commenting, "I love George, and I'm pretty sure he loves me. But, you know what? Sometimes I wonder. After all, he's never really *done* anything that makes me believe that he feels the same way."

How can Christy so easily overlook George's actions and gestures? They are so obviously intended to make her life easier and clearly show that this is a man who cares for her deeply and is planning for their shared future.

I know that if I were regularly helping out my in-laws and then having my time and efforts so easily and quickly dismissed, I would feel pretty upset. I can only imagine how George feels when Christy doesn't appreciate his loving gestures.

While Christy's obliviousness to George's efforts may jump right off the page to you and me, I'm quite sure that Christy is genuinely blind to this reality. And I'm equally sure that most women, myself very much included here, have been in Christy's shoes: overlooking the day-to-day gestures that our boyfriends or partners make to show their love and try to make us happy.

Quick quiz: Which is more romantic—avoiding fancy dinners to pay off someone else's loan or giving someone Hallmark cards and boxes of Godiva chocolates?

Think about it. Just because George isn't using rose petals, champagne, or other clichés to express himself doesn't mean he isn't seriously in love with Christy and committed to her. I think his personal gestures have much more meaning than any heart-shaped box of chocolates.

Of course everyone likes flowers and candy now and then, but I've found that since my son was born, one of the most romantic things my husband does for me is to run me a bath (that I can enjoy alone!), order some food in, and then take night duty while I snuggle up (alone!) in our spare bedroom and enjoy a luxurious eight hours of uninterrupted sleep. Hardly the stuff of romance novels. But the truth is, nothing else could make me feel better or more cherished.

Anna, a plain-speaking 34-year-old nurse, complains that Jim, her boyfriend of almost a year, "wouldn't know romance if it came up, introduced itself, and then hit him over the head!" Anna has very clear and definite ideas of romance (and, I suspect, everything else!). "Flowers, candles, fire, small tables at fancy bistros, walks on the beach. . . ." But when I ask her *why* she wants those things and what makes those particular examples the definition of romance in her mind, she dismisses the questions with a huge laugh. "Please, now you sound like Jim!" she says.

Like most of us, Anna's views and expectations around romance have been created by someone else, and whether she realizes it or not, she's simply accepted them as her own. Along the way, she's transferred all the accompanying expectations to her boyfriend Jim. If he doesn't know the "right" romantic moves to make, Anna feels disappointed. And equally, if she feels that she has to prompt him to do what she wants, then somehow, it no longer "counts."

Where do these rigid views and expectations about romance come from? A big part of the blame lies with the pervasive media and marketing images that surround us. As I've discussed several times already, these images that we've seen practically from birth combine to create our definitions and expectations of what is romantic and how it should look. The result is that, like Christy and Anna, our expectations of how love should be expressed are completely distorted and not based on reality. When you really think about it, it's actually kind of sad that we've narrowed down our definitions of romance and love to such a limited set of images and actions that have nothing to do with our individual partners or relationships.

No One Does It Like De Beers

In her book *The Meaning of Wife*, Anne Kingston describes how one of the most impressive manipulations of our feelings about love and romance comes from De Beers. This company transformed a common, overmined gem into our ultimate symbol of eternal love and romance. Here's how.

De Beers was founded in 1871 by Sir Cecil Rhodes as a way of regulating the huge diamond deposit that was discovered in South Africa (which contained 90 percent of the world's diamond supply). To make money, Rhodes knew that manipulating supply wasn't enough; he also had to stimulate demand. One (very successful) part of his strategy was to create a market for diamond engagement rings in North America.

In 1938, a New York advertising firm was given the brief to essentially, "make diamonds an inseparable part of courtship and married life in North America." The goal was to instill the idea in people that diamonds possessed an emotional value that exceeded their market worth. As well, the idea was to have diamonds be viewed as a lifetime object, so people wouldn't try to resell them and increase the supply.

In 1948, copywriter Frances Gerety (a woman who, incidentally, never married) came up with the now ubiquitous tagline, "A diamond is forever," a line that *Advertising Age* proclaimed the greatest advertising slogan of the twentieth century.

De Beers then cleverly went on to link the "value" of the future wife directly to her husband's earning potential by promoting the idea that an engagement ring should cost two months of her future husband's salary. This was done through ads that said: "You can't look at Jane and tell me she's not worth two months' salary. Just look at her. So I wanted to get her the biggest diamond I could afford. One that other men could see without getting too close."

Interestingly, the cost of love varied around the world—or more specifically, the number of months' salary that is promoted as being the required norm changes depending on what local markets would bear. For instance, in Europe, men were asked to pony up the equivalent of one month's salary. In Japan, it was three months'.

De Beers also got involved with helping plan how engagements happen, finding numerous ways to promote the "romantic" surprise proposal. Why? Well, it has nothing to do with the company just being helpful and everything to do with their bottom line. They positioned surprise proposals as the more romantic option, since the company's research revealed that if women picked their own engagement ring, they tended to spend less than if their fiancé chose the gem on his own. And thus (giving romantic movies the ending we all wait for!) was born the idea that a romantic proposal is defined by the man already having the ring in hand. I'm sure you won't be surprised to learn that the De Beers website even used to offer engagement proposal ideas.

So, the next time you find yourself dreaming of a rock on your finger (or wishing the one your husband had bought was a little bigger), remember, it has nothing do to with love and everything to do with the business objectives of Sir Cecil Rhodes.

Please don't get me wrong; there's nothing bad about liking roses and champagne. Who wouldn't? The problem occurs when we believe that love, romance, or a happy marriage should *look* a certain way to be real, or when our expectations and desires come from outside sources, like Hallmark or De Beers, instead of from within our partners or ourselves.

The result is that we put our happiness on hold or fail to enjoy what is real and happening at the moment and all around us—all because it doesn't match the fairy tale picture of our fantasies. But have you ever felt unsatisfied by a romantic gesture that felt hollow? One woman told me of receiving a dozen long-stem red roses on Valentines' Day . . . after her boyfriend called to cancel their dinner because he had to work late. Another told me of a "perfect" tasting-menu dinner with wine accompaniment that was one of her worst dates because the guy was more interested in impressing her with his gourmet knowledge than in actually listening to anything she had to say.

Or, have you had a situation that felt utterly romantic because it was so suited to your own quirky view of happiness? One friend loves to tell me about the time her boyfriend brought her a case of Diet Coke and two boxes of graham crackers (her favorite study snack) while she was cramming for an exam in college. He didn't want to interrupt her studying, so he rang the doorbell and ran away, leaving her the treats with a sweet good luck note.

But some women still feel disappointed when they don't receive the goodies they want from a romantic partner. So instead of enjoying what they have, they focus on trying to fix it so it resembles our mythical images and ingrained beliefs around romance.

That's what happened with 29-year-old Hannah and her ex-boyfriend Scott. "When Scott moved two hours away for a new job, I was upset, of course, but a part of me was really excited about the weekends we would have together. My roommate in college had a long-distance relationship for the last two years, and it always seemed so romantic to me. They would both put in so much effort for the times that they saw each other—like planning little surprises, making sure they both dressed up and looked their best."

The reality for Hannah and Scott was nothing like that. "I admit I had high expectations; I thought he should be going all out for me with really nice dates on the weekend since he didn't get to see me all week." Scott, on the other hand, just wanted to relax with Hannah at home. "Eventually we got into a routine where I would come up to his place Friday night after work, all dressed up and excited, and he would be sitting there exhausted, looking at takeout menus. I'd be frustrated and disappointed, and it would spiral down from there.

"You know, looking back, I realize that Scott was making an effort. I mean, he always hated the phone when we both lived in Chicago, but when we were far apart he made a big effort to call and be chatty on the phone, and send me texts and e-mails during the day. And you know what? It wasn't that it wasn't enough, it's that it wasn't what I had already decided I wanted in my head and was waiting for him make happen for me. It sounds crazy now, but that's what I wanted. Even though Scott had no idea about my old roommate or what I was secretly expecting."

And that's where the real issue is and why romance needs a rewrite! Too many of us, influenced by books, movies, and advertising (and even stories from girlfriends who've had a romantic experience or two), are walking around with fixed ideas in our heads of what romance is or should be when it's with our Mr. Right. So we keep waiting for a man to come along who somehow knows how to make the script in our minds come to life. And if the guy doesn't live up to this fantasy, then he's clearly not our soul mate and maybe we should hold out for someone else.

The other problem with our fixation is the heavy weight of expectations this creates. Think of that panic or duty feeling that so many people feel around Valentine's Day, birthdays, and anniversaries—and the sort of exhaustion that follows these "big dates" when couples bicker simply from the pressure of having to live up to it all. How romantic is that really?

Ask yourself this: do you really want candlelit dinners for two or do you think you *should* want that? Or, even worse: do most women want such things just so we can compare and share such stories with our friends, to see whose partner is winning the romance olympics?

Exercise: True Romance

———◦∿◦———

It might surprise you to realize how powerful fairy tales, movies, and marketing images really are in determining your definition of romance. But there is nothing that says you are not allowed to write your *own* definition, so, go for it! Here's your chance to define romance for yourself, once and for all. What do you *really* want your partner to do on a daily basis or on special occasions to show his love? What *really* makes you feel adored? Consider your answers to the following questions.

1. Describe your ideal first date with a new man or a date with your current partner. Where do you go? What do you do together? Are you outdoors? Is it in the afternoon? Does it involve champagne? Hamburgers? Chocolate? Frisbee? Candles? Backgammon? Flowers? How would such date make you feel? Would it be planned so you could look forward to it, or would you prefer to be surprised?

2. How would you feel about not doing or getting anything for Valentine's Day—honestly?

3. What gift(s) would you most like to receive from a partner?

4. What would your ideal marriage proposal involve? Where would you be and what would happen?

Hint: If after doing this list you realize that you know what you really want, then why not share your desires with your partner? Letting go of the idea that your man should somehow "just know" what you want—when, in most cases, men have no idea—means that you have a better chance of getting the attention, gifts, and happiness you desire. I have a feeling your man will thank you for the guidance.

Is This Love . . . or Competition?

Sally, a 36-year-old lab technician in Florida, was telling me about a situation that is probably far more common than most of us are willing to admit. What happened to her was that after several of her friends and coworkers all started dating new men around the same time, she began to feel as though they were all "competitively dating."

"It was like we were all trying to be the happier, closer, more romantic couple. Soon, I started to feel like Greg and I weren't doing enough together." Even when they first started dating, Sally and Greg had always been really low-key and casual about the time they spent together, enjoying just sitting outside and having a couple of beers or maybe going for a walk. But now Sally started planning more "romantic activities" and pressuring Greg to do the same, even though both of them had been happy with the way things were before.

"I started booking all these big nights out and dinners with elaborate menus, and Greg hated it. Instead of being a fun, re-laxed time together, it would be like this chore that we'd both be gearing ourselves up for. And at the end of the evening, I always felt disappointed by the way it had gone—not to mention all the money we'd spent. It would feel like a waste since the evening never turned out to be what I'd been hoping for or picturing. But at least it gave me something to share with everyone at work the next day."

The problem with having all these fixed ideas or rules about what romance is or how love should be expressed is that it essentially creates a completely artificial set of requirements that must be met. All the individuality is removed, and, essentially, it just sets a couple up for disappointment.

The Arranged Marriage Way:
Romance Has Any Definition You Choose

By their very nature, arranged marriages don't fit into any of the models or narratives of romance shown in advertising and popular culture. In fact, let's be honest, most people probably think of arranged marriage as the polar opposite of romance!

Since the couple in an arranged marriage are usually brought together by the two families, there's obviously no dating or romantic marriage proposal, and even if the prospective bride and groom are involved in the match, they certainly don't know each other well enough to engage in actions or activities that fall into what we would consider to be romantic.

In traditional arranged marriages, particularly those from our grandparents' generation, the future bride and groom rarely met before the actual wedding. Instead of an engagement as we think of it, there was usually some sort of ceremony between the two families where gifts were exchanged to mark the occasion. In more recent arranged marriages, like that of my parents, the couple did meet at the engagement ceremony, although they were married two weeks later.

Today, couples in an arranged marriage generally attend an engagement ceremony to mark the occasion, and, although the man doesn't actually propose (since it's all been decided already), modern culture has found its way into the process. Brides today do wear an engagement ring (usually a gift from the man's family as part of her wedding jewelry). However, the potential for traditional romance is essentially nonexistent, since most of this engagement activity happens in the presence of family, friends, and, depending on cultural and religious backgrounds, priests as well.

All of this probably leads you to conclude that romance is pretty nonexistent in an arranged marriage.

Well, yes and no. As we've been discussing, this all depends on your definition of romance. I admit that during my first few interviews, I was genuinely surprised when women started to tell me that, yes, they did find their husbands romantic.

Now, I have to be honest here. I'd grown up around arranged marriages that seemed quite happy, so I suspected that there was more to it than I understood or had been led to believe by the common portrayal of them. So it wasn't a complete surprise to come across some really positive aspects of arranged marriage during my initial interviews—but I really hadn't thought that romance would be among them.

The problem was that I, even with my knowledge of arranged marriages, was seeing and defining "romance" by our standard narrow cultural parameters. I hadn't yet realized that romance could and actually should come in many different forms. For one thing, I came into the interviews thinking that if you weren't in love when you got married, you couldn't possibly have romance. I learned very quickly that this is not so. If anything, coming into a relationship without preconceived ideas of marital love means that you have more freedom to enjoy romance on your own terms that you decide together.

It was Ritu, the 62-year-old mother of four adult sons, who set me straight. Over tea in her kitchen, I questioned her about whether she thought she really had romance in her marriage.

Ritu and Anil had never met when they married over forty years ago in Delhi. His family knew hers and approached them about a match when she was still in school.

"When I was sixteen and he was eighteen, our parents agreed to our engagement. At the time neither of us thought much about it. We were both away at boarding school and busy. But gradually, each time I went home, my mother would tell me stories about how clever he was or how well he and his cricket team had done, and gradually I started thinking more about him, even though I didn't actually know him."

Although their parents were friends, Ritu and Anil still didn't meet until their wedding day. Soon after, they moved to California, and then to Canada for Anil's job in academics. "We were so young then, but so happy," she remembers. "It was like playing house together. Every little thing was so new and exciting.

"My sons are like you," she snorts derisively. "They think that because they don't see their father carrying bunches of flowers home or giving me big presents in front of them, it means that we don't have any romance in our marriage. Fools!"

As my conversations continued with other women in arranged marriages, I began to learn what so many of these women had intuited early in their relationships: romance comes in many forms and each person expresses it differently. And sometimes, having romance in your marriage is about learning to recognize it.

"It doesn't have to look like what you see on TV," laughs 53-year-old Christiana, from the West Indies. "I don't look like what you see on TV!"

This theme came up throughout my interviews, that, yes, women in arranged marriages did think that they have developed genuine romance in their relationships. But the examples they gave weren't the ones sold to us by Madison Avenue or profiled by *People*. Instead, they were ones that that I now consider my standard for genuine romance—gestures that didn't necessarily involve lots of money or flash, but that in some way genuinely convey a thoughtfulness or sweetness and often seem to require some attention to be noticed and fully appreciated. They are also gestures that show a genuine knowledge of the person they are meant to please.

Real Romance

These expressions of love might not look like the Hallmark ads, but here are some examples of some of my interviewees' definitions of romance:

- "I was really nervous about driving for the first ten years of marriage, so my husband would wake up at five thirty in the morning to drive me across town for my seven o'clock shift before coming back to get the kids and himself ready."

  —Sheila, 41

- "After my sister's husband died, he invited her to come live with us and then helped pay for her son to go to university."

  —Praveena, 56

- "He took a second job on the evenings and weekends so we could afford the house I really wanted."

  —Rani, 33

- "He started to read all my favorite novels, particularly the ones I liked growing up, so we could talk about them."

  —Anooja, 36

- "He's brought me a cup of hot tea in bed every Saturday and Sunday since the first week we were married."

  —Amarit, 44

Couples in arranged marriages can't really identify with any of the cultural or marketing images around what romance or love should be like since it just doesn't work with their own story and experience. As a result, they develop their own rituals, traditions, and interpretations of romance as they get to know each other over the course of their marriage.

By not accepting prescribed, "popular" definitions of how love and affection should be expressed, women in arranged marriages tend to have a much easier time both recognizing and enjoying the more individual romantic gestures of their partners. They look for the things that we might not notice and choose to see them as proof of love and romance.

One woman, Abba, who was in her late fifties, told me that when she decided to go back to school in her late thirties—after almost seventeen years of marriage—her husband learned how to cook so he could help out in the evenings while she was in class. I think she must have sensed that I wasn't overly impressed by this gesture, because she tried to make me understand why this meant so much to her. "Men in those days, especially if you were raised in India, never learned how to cook. Most of them rarely even stepped into the kitchen. When he started to learn to cook proper Indian food, so that we could still eat what we liked without adding to my workload, I was so impressed and touched."

And that's the key point: it's not about what anyone else thinks of a particular gesture; all that matters is that it means something to the two people in the relationship. In fact, I was very impressed by Abba's husband's gesture. I'd rather have my husband cook for me than a bunch of flowers or a dinner out any day!

So how is it that women in arranged marriages are able to clearly see that romance does not have to be narrowly defined? Because they enter the relationship with fewer expectations about romance. If their partner's actions or the pattern and tone of their relationship don't seem to be fitting into the cultural stereotype of romance, this doesn't seem like something is wrong or needs to be fixed. It's all about expectations, and keeping them realistic.

Since arranged marriages are not based on love (at least not in the beginning), they are essentially the opposite of our relationships. They don't start with romance; instead, romance—however the couple defines it—develops later in the relationship as the couple gets to know each other and as time passes, when it's needed even more. This again shows the value of complete commitment: when you are totally committed to a relationship, you give yourself more time to discover what makes the other person happy and don't need to use gifts and surprises such as flowers, champagne, and chocolate.

In contrast, love marriages tend to have all the intensity, excitement, and romance at the beginning of the relationship. Once the honeymoon period of wine and roses inevitably turns into regular everyday life, there is an even greater pressure for big romantic gestures to somehow counter what is actually a natural relationship shift—a shift that is rarely portrayed in the media. Since the arranged-marriage model is also never really shown in popular culture and media (and certainly not glamorized or idealized), the men and women in them don't have the sense of trying to duplicate a certain approved way of loving. There are no rules. This is freeing. Luckily, by reading this book, you can enjoy this freedom as well.

One of the best examples of how expectations in an arranged marriage change everything is Shoba's story. Now 34, she is the ex-girlfriend of a close friend of mine, Irwin. At the time Shoba and my friend were together, she was living in Denver. Although she was studying creative writing at the local university, her real focus, or so it seemed, was driving my friend Irwin crazy.

Shoba used to proudly describe herself as a "princess" and "high maintenance." Irwin, a busy radiologist, found that he could never seem to make her happy. She believed he was completely responsible for knowing what she was in the mood to do and whether she had a good time at an evening out and for indulging all of her many attendant concerns and issues. While they were together, we got used to Irwin never really being present at a dinner or evening out for drinks since, if she wasn't there, she would call and need him to spend the rest of the evening talking to her. Not surprisingly, after about a year and a half, he ended the relationship. Soon after we heard that she had had an arranged marriage to the son of one her father's colleagues. Everyone who had ever seen them together felt sympathy for the poor man!

Two years later I ran into Shoba at a beach resort in south India (proving that the world is so much smaller than we think). She was there with her husband and looked as glamorous as I remembered. But after watching her with him for a couple of days, I noticed that she was acting completely differently. She seemed calmer, more relaxed, less demanding. Even my husband—never her biggest fan—had to acknowledge the obvious change. We decided it had to be result of age, but I wondered: could two years really make such a difference? I had to find out. Over a few cocktails one afternoon, I started asking Shoba how her arranged marriage was different than her relationship with Irwin. Bolstered by the rum punch we were drinking, I delicately suggested that she seemed a lot easier on her husband than she ever had been with Irwin.

"That was different," she said. "Irwin was for fun. I mean, we met randomly on the beach! He was the one always talking about how he saw me and knew we were soul mates, so he had to do those things. But with Shiv [her new husband], it's different; even I don't expect all that!"

Shoba's story shows us that when women go into an arranged marriage their expectations change, and so does their ability to create their own definitions of happiness and romance. As Shoba's dramatic change of behavior reveals, when it's "love" or a fun relationship, there is a greater sense that the other person should be able to provide an unrealistic level of romance and understanding.

With her arranged marriage, Shoba became much more realistic about her expectations of her partner's actions, patience, and feelings. By changing her expectations of her husband, Shoba is not setting him up to feel frustrated by his inability to please her the way she did with Irwin. Rather, she takes a long-term, day-to-day view and she is content.

One of the funniest people I spoke with was an older Greek woman who had an arranged marriage decades earlier, before she and her husband moved to a New York suburb. She told me a story about how her 27-year-old granddaughter had come over upset that her boyfriend hadn't planned or done anything special for Valentine's Day. The woman didn't understand what the problem was at all. "So, he forgets to buy a card one day? I know him; he's a good boy and he's good to you every day. Why get so mad about this one day?"

As you can see, our expectations about what defines love determine how happy we are in our relationships. Women in arranged marriages or those who approach relationships the arranged-marriage way don't unthinkingly buy into what society tells us that men need to do to make us happy. We decide that for ourselves, and thus we don't worry about things that aren't really important.

All of which means, it's time for a serious rewrite on romance!

Let's forget all the hyped-up expectations and narrow definitions that are just causing chaos in our dating lives and undermining our personal happiness and relationship confidence. Why let marketing and advertising executives or troubled celebrities set the standard for what romance is or a relationship should look like? It's all about what makes *you* feel happy and cherished and the individual way that the men you meet choose to express that to you. Think of what a glorious world of joy awaits you beyond the unoriginality of flowers and chocolate!

A happy relationship is not only something each us *can* define for ourselves; it's something we *must* define for ourselves. And when we do, we free ourselves from the pressure to pursue perfection, free ourselves from competition with other relationships, free ourselves from getting angry at our partners every time they don't conform to what society tells us a "loving partner" should be. Basically, we become free from putting our happiness on hold and allow ourselves to experience happiness, love, and intimacy beyond anything we've ever seen in a magazine.

And you know what? It's change that a man will sense in you. Men who care about you just want to make you happy, and the more open you are to different expressions of love and caring, the happier you will be. The more specific you can be about what pleases you, the more he can give that exact thing or feeling or emotion to you. It's really that simple: decide what you want romance to be and then ask for it.

While your partner will and should take into account how you view romance (after all, he wants you to be happy), it's equally important that you don't just look for and count the big, obvious gestures. Instead, find more regular happiness and love by paying attention to the smaller, day-to-day, and often more genuine romantic actions that are happening around you. Take time to notice all the little things a man does to make you happy, whether it's picking up your favorite ice-cream flavor or handing you the best section of the weekend paper first.

Changing how you define romance will change both your

expectations and your experiences when it comes to dating. You will no longer have the limiting beliefs that come from buying into the outside rules of what love and romance need to be. This means dating will become easier, and more enjoyable, since your only criteria for what is romantic is what makes *you* feel loved. You will be aware of the different ways men express love, and learn about what gestures really make you the most happy and fulfilled. This will also help you *finally* get rid of that feeling that no man ever lives up to the fantasy in your head. Instead, you can start actually enjoying what you have!

Living This Secret

- **Don't believe the hype.** Don't let Hollywood, the media, or anyone else define what romance means. Romance comes in many forms and each person expresses it differently.

- **Define romance for you and your partner.** Remember that our general image of romance is a creation of our culture. People in other cultures don't have the same expectations of their relationships. This means you can—and should—define romance, love, and a happy relationship on your own terms.

- **Cherish the small stuff.** Little expressions of love over time add up to more romance than any box of chocolates. Notice nice gestures when you go on a first date. Pay attention and appreciate everything. When you're in a relationship, don't wait until Valentine's Day to notice a partner's loving acts—and to make your own.

Chapter Six

Secret #6

His Sex Appeal?
It's All About You!

Find Personal Satisfaction by
Paying Attention to the Positives

Jill likes to explain her turbulent and dramatic sex life by saying that she's a Taurus, so she just can't help being led by what she describes as "the sensual side" of her personality.

Since I first met Jill over six years ago, I've heard this line quite a few times. Tiny, with delicate features and short dark hair, 34-year-old Jill is an incredible commercial law litigator. Organized and focused, she seems to have everything but her romantic life under control.

Since the first time we went for drinks and bonded over our mutual man problems, Jill has been entertaining me with stories that sound straight out of the pages of *Cosmo*—with Jill playing a central role in a series of wild escapades that range from her leaving a dinner date to hook up with their waiter during his break to meeting a man on the subway, taking time off work, and spending an intense, all-consuming three weeks holed up with him in his studio apartment. Not the kind of stuff that you share with Mom!

But Jill's excitement and energy for her random adventures is starting to disappear, and instead, for the past couple of years, she has started talking about wanting to meet someone special and settle down.

While it's not the first time I've heard this from her, this time it—and she—seem different. For the first time since I've known her, Jill is making a big effort to meet someone a bit more suitable for something more serious. Her plan has included getting her friends to set her up and even joining a once-a-month singles dining club for lawyers.

"It's not that I'm interested in getting married right now, but I think I'm ready for someone to have a few regular nights with, someone who's interesting to talk to and easy to just relax with," she says. It doesn't sound like much to ask, does it? But as you've probably guessed, Jill has a tendency to end up in intense, highly passionate, and generally inappropriate flings or affairs.

Other than the sex, it's difficult to find anything that Jill and her dates have in common—or even really like about each other. So once the initial spark burns itself out, the relationship usually comes to an abrupt and dramatic end.

At times, I admit that it's hard not to be a little envious of Jill's adventures. This is particularly true on days when I'm feeling slightly frumpy, plodding through a flannel-pajamas-who-cares-about-getting-my-legs-waxed marriage day, and she is literally glowing from being up all night having incredible sex with some guy she hadn't seen in months. But the feelings of envy usually end when she tells me that he's been in rehab for the past few months.

After years of stories like this, there's also a sense of genuine concern since Jill never seems to get involved with anyone who appears to have any of the qualities of a decent boyfriend, let alone a husband! Bankruptcy, drugs, wives, girlfriends, and even jail—over the past six years I seem to have heard them all. The sex may be hot, but generally everything else about these men is not.

I think that Jill genuinely does want to move on. As she explains it, "Of course, I'd like to meet someone that I could at least mention in my weekly calls home. Forget taking him home, I'd like to just start with that!

"It's not like I choose these guys," Jill explains defensively. "Clearly, I would love to be passionately attracted to a caring banker or doctor who's in his thirties, single and substance-free. And I do keep trying to meet these guys, but you can't control who you are attracted to, and it just seems that these are the men I meet and have chemistry with, and in situations like that, there's just nothing else you can do but go for it."

Although maybe not quite as dramatically as Jill, many of us over the course of our dating adventures have had some experience with the feeling of being completely and totally caught up in an affair—a feeling of sexual attraction that just seems to make no sense to you or anyone who knows you. You forget your usual responsibilities and let everything else slide (after all, nothing matters but being together). You don't need sleep or food and yet have probably never looked better.

Nothing else matters but you and the other person. There is no obstacle that can't be conquered. Who cares if he's not what you're looking for or already involved with another woman? You're convinced that this must be the real thing and, just like in songs, feel ready to give anything up or do whatever it takes to be together. It feels amazing, doesn't it?

And then it ends. And suddenly even thinking of about him leaves you cold and genuinely wondering what that was all about, what you thought you saw in him and why you acted like that. As a life experience it's great, but as a way of life, it most definitely is not.

The Science of Sexual Chemistry

As unromantic as it sounds, according to anthropologist Helen Fisher, author of *Anatomy of Love* (a study of adultery, monogamy, and divorce throughout history), the intense and overwhelming feelings we experience with initial attraction are nothing more than a chemical reaction within our own brains. Fisher writes: "This violent emotional disturbance that we call infatuation (or attraction) may begin with a small molecule called phenylethylamine, or PEA. PEA is the substance in the brain that causes feelings of elation, exhilaration, euphoria." She estimates that the normal duration of the infatuation stage is two to three years. After surveying the pattern of divorce statistics in sixty-two cultures, Fisher found that the peak time for a couple to divorce tends to be in the fourth year of the relationship.

Germaine Greer, feminist icon and author of *The Female Eunuch,* would agree with this view of what love is. In the book's chapter on obsession, Greer compares being in love to being "in pain, in shock, in trouble. The love object occupies the thoughts of the person. . . . Expectations are set up which no human being could possibly fulfill. . . . The impotence of will and rationality to deal with this mania is recognized in the common terms *madly, wildly, deliriously, head-over-heels* in love, since it would be oxymoronic to claim to be gently, reliably or sensibly in love."

Now, let's look at the flip side of superintense sexual attraction. Even more common among the women I interviewed was the experience of meeting someone who seems perfect in every way, but you just don't feel attracted to him. He might be intelligent and thoughtful, with a great sense of humor—everything you said you've been looking for in a man—and he might even meet all your marriage musts. But you just don't feel that spark, and because you feel no intense chemistry, you end the relationship. Then, a few months or bad dates later, you start wondering why you didn't give Mr. No Chemistry a bit more of a chance.

Becca, a 37-year-old advertising executive, remembers. "When I first met Adam at a friend's housewarming, he honestly didn't even register on my radar. He was shorter than the men I was usually attracted to and I was far more into the hot friend he was with." A week later, when Adam e-mailed her for a coffee (having gotten her details from the housewarming e-vite), she went out with him. "But honestly, it was partly because I couldn't remember which one he was and because it was an empty Sunday afternoon and I didn't have anything going on anyway!"

To her complete surprise, Becca had a great time with Adam. "He was really funny and super interesting. Adam's a screen-writer who also does some television work, and after our three-hour coffee, I thought that I definitely wanted to be friends with this man. But there was still no physical attraction for me."

Still, Becca met up with him again, and this time, they had a few drinks and a four-hour chat session, during which "I told him straight out that I didn't find him attractive, that he wasn't my type, and that nothing romantic would ever develop between us." Not surprisingly, Adam didn't call again.

Becca went back to dating. "I never believed that you could grow to be attracted to someone. To me it was just pretty clear-cut, you were or you weren't attracted; anything else just seemed like you were settling." Becca didn't see Adam again for seven months. During that time, she met and dated a few other guys whom she thought she was attracted to, but admits her mind just kept going back to Adam.

Finally, she called him and they arranged to meet. The Hollywood ending to their story would be that when she saw him this time, the months apart would have made her completely and utterly attracted to him. Becca laughs. "I wish! No, it wasn't like I was suddenly superattracted to him, but more like I was just deeply happy to see him." Contrary to what she had always previously thought, genuine attraction really did follow, and two years later, they are engaged and planning an April wedding on an island in the Caribbean. "Adam's still not my 'type,' whatever that means, but I still get so nervous thinking about how close I almost came to losing him forever!" Just as with love, sexual attraction is something that we've been conditioned to think of as being completely beyond our control. Well, guess what? It isn't. Like love and commitment, attraction is a choice you can make. It can grow, and you can control how and when it happens. Arranged marriages prove this.

You might be mentally going over the men in your life, whether past or present, and thinking, well, yeah, that would be nice. And like Jill, you may be thinking that obviously if you *could,* you *would* control who you were attracted to. But how can you?

Well, try this theory on for size: Your feelings of attraction toward a guy have much more to do with *you* than they do with the looks, personality, or sex appeal of that guy. (Well, maybe not when it comes to George Clooney, but with just about everyone else!)

Love at Second Sight

This theory definitely hits home for 35-year-old Carol, a policy adviser at a think tank in New York. "The first time I met Graham, I'd just come from a day spent struggling to write a section of my thesis. The only reason I left the house is that I'd promised my friend a couple of months ago that I'd come to her dinner and I knew she'd go crazy if I was a no-show. After a week of erratic sleeping, no gym, and a diet of bagels, Red Bull, and Cheetos, I felt disgusting. Not surprisingly, when Karen seated me next to Graham, I was completely indifferent to him. Thinking back, I was probably a complete bitch! When my friend Karen casually asked me what I thought of him, my instant response was, "What? Who?"

Five months later, Carol and Graham ran into each other at a friend's engagement party. This time, Carol was in a completely different frame of mind. "I felt great! I'd just had a haircut and was wearing a new sundress when Graham came over to say hi. It was like meeting a whole different person and this time we completely clicked. At the end of the night, he walked me out to get a cab, we kissed, exchanged numbers, and have been dating ever since!"

So what changed? When Carol tells the story, how Graham looked the second time she saw him doesn't even play into it. Instead, it's all about how she felt about herself, and what she looked like that seems to have changed how he she felt about him.

See if you can apply this principle to your own life. Think about a time when:

- You were feeling your most attractive—at a party, a wedding, a work event, anywhere—and the event suddenly seemed full of attractive men with lots of possibility!

- You were feeling really confident—thanks to a big win at work, a new haircut, or even a few cocktails—and suddenly every guy in the room wanted to talk to you

- You felt grumpy and unattractive, you were having a bad hair day or wearing clothes that didn't suit you—and somehow that day there just seemed to be no attractive men on the planet

I would argue that in every single one of these situations, the attractiveness and attention of the men was entirely based on you—your feelings about yourself and the energy you were sending out. How you feel sexually and physically about a particular man is more influenced by our own feelings than we ever acknowledge. The guys don't change; we do.

If you approach your life and relationships from a spiritual perspective, this point is driven home by popular author Deepak Chopra in his book *The Path to Love.* As Chopra says, finding love is about finding yourself.

> People today are consumed by doubts about their relationships: Have I found the right partner? Am I being true to myself? Have I given the best part of myself away? As a result, there is a restless kind of consumer shopping for partners, as if the "right" one can be found by toting up a potential mate's pluses and minuses until the number of pluses matches some mythical standard. The path to love, however, is never about externals. However good or bad you feel about your relationship, the person you are with at this moment is the "right" person, because he or she is a mirror of who you are inside. . . . When you struggle with your partner, you are struggling with yourself. Every fault you see in them touches a denied weakness in yourself. Every conflict you wage is an excuse not to face a conflict within. The path to love therefore clears up a monumental mistake that millions of people make—the mistake that someone "out there" is going to give (or take) something that is not already yours. When you truly find love, you find yourself.

The Elspeth Effect

Still not convinced?

Meet Whitley and her husband, Roger, a couple who, on first meeting, seem completely mismatched. She's tall and model-thin and always looks perfectly put together regardless of the time of day or what's going on her life. Her husband is the opposite: almost a head shorter and thirty-plus pounds overweight. Roger didn't even look pulled together on their wedding day! I'll be honest; whenever I see them together, even five years into the marriage, their pairing still strikes me as weird.

"I knew Roger for three years before we ever got together. He was always sort of there, around me, but he was the last person that I would ever have even considered dating." Those were three extremely tumultuous years in Whitley's life, though. Her brother was in a serious car accident, her business went through severe financial difficulties, and she finally ended a decade-long on-and-off-again relationship. "Through all of this Roger was always there for me, just as a friend, but I gradually found myself turning to him more and more if I needed someone to talk to, or to help me with something. The accident really made me realize that too often, when we need our friends the most, they just don't seem able to deliver. It was the opposite with Roger, though. He's never once let me down."

Roger and Whitley never officially started dating. After three years of spending more and more time together, they finally kissed one night. A year later they were married.

As someone who was aware of their relationship from the sidelines, I saw that what changed over those years was what Whitley noticed and focused on about Roger. Eventually, this changed how she felt about him, although Roger himself didn't actually change at all!

Most of us have been conditioned to accept the disempowering belief that sexual chemistry either exists or it doesn't, and that you "know" from the minute you first catch eyes with someone whether it's there or not. It's actually quite sad to think of how many potentially good relationships, like Whitley and Roger's, have never had a chance even to begin as a result of this limiting belief. To put it bluntly, looks just don't matter that much when it comes to finding a great mate. Attraction and attractiveness are all in your mind.

One of my favorite examples of how outside factors change what we notice or how we feel is what my friends and I call the "Elspeth effect." Elspeth has been a friend of mine since junior high school. Over the many, many years that I've known her, I've met or known most of the men that she's been involved with. But even when we were in high school, the Elspeth effect was very much in evidence.

What do I mean by this? Well, Elspeth would start dating a guy whom we'd all also met or known but had never considered in "that way" before because he was too quiet, not athletic enough, had bad skin, or simply was not sexy. Once the particular guy was dating Elspeth, though, suddenly we'd all be asking ourselves why we hadn't noticed him before, especially when he was so *obviously* cute, charming, interesting, had all the perfect qualities of a boyfriend . . . you get the idea. It wasn't that Elspeth actually changed the guy in any physical or tangible way—well, maybe the odd haircut or wardrobe update—but it was more that our perceptions changed. Once they had the Elspeth effect, we'd all start looking at the guys differently and wishing we had noticed them first.

Remember Those Marriage Musts

In my opinion, the reason the above relationships work comes back to the concept of marriage musts. You just can't go back out there into the dating world without really getting clear on what yours are and why they matter to you.

So if you haven't done them, go back to Chapter 2 and make that list. And even if you have, just to reinforce them, write them out again in your journal or elsewhere. I even encourage you to prioritize them with a short sentence about *why* each is important for you.

In Chapter 3 we talked about escaping the trap of the "type" to look beyond any preconceived ideas about who might be right for you and instead focus on your marriage musts.

Once you have your marriage musts clear, you can more easily look beyond height, weight, hair color, eye color, athletic ability, and pretty much any other physical characteristic. As women in arranged marriages know, all of these surface traits pale in comparison to the marriage musts when it comes to lifelong happiness. For a moment, let's think about the opposite side of this coin. As many of our grandmothers have told us for years, beauty fades. This means *our* beauty will fade as well. Do you want a man to marry you for your looks, weight, or other physical quality or because of who you are deep down inside?

It's All About You

The bottom line: sexual attraction to a man—any man—is far more under your control than you probably realize. Feelings of love and lust are influenced by how you feel about yourself, the timing in your life, the environment you're in, your mood, your attitude, and your energy far more than his height, smile, sense of humor, or sexual prowess.

What it comes down to is this: your sexual attraction to a man is about you. It's a simple idea, but it takes a while to get used to. Once you do, you'll see it's both incredibly powerful and incredibly liberating. In fact, the power of your personal circumstances to influence your feelings of attraction to a man is one of the reasons that many dating and introduction agencies require clients to commit to attending at least two dates before deciding how they feel—because they know that various internal factors influence how attractive we find someone else.

So, if sexual chemistry can be manipulated like that, then why aren't we trying to be even slightly strategic about it? Well, some people are trying to teach this lesson. In *Mama Gena's Owner's and Operator's Guide to Men,* Regena Thomashauer writes:

> A loving relationship begins with self-love. Instead of examining, in microscopic detail, what you do not have, try learning about what you have. Instead of criticizing your body, your beauty, your decisions, try appreciating them. . . . I want you to become as comfortable with pleasure as you are with pain.

Take a page from Mama Gena and other sensuality gurus. Love yourself the way you want a man to love you. Send yourself flowers, take yourself to your favorite restaurant, compliment yourself in the mirror. The more attractive you feel, the more attractive you will be to men. It's really that simple.

Why It's So Hard to Put Sex in Perspective

Maybe one of the reasons that we are all so focused on sexual chemistry is that we are basically sex-obsessed as a society. It's no secret that sex sells—everything from liquor to laptops to lawn furniture—and virtually every issue of every women's magazine ever created!

I am certainly not going to tell you that sex isn't important, or fabulous, or a component of a strong and lasting relationship—because it is! But I am going to tell you that, contrary to what many advertisements, films, and TV shows often promote—and what many women falsely believe—sex is not the central focus of a relationship.

Sex is just one factor among many that make a relationship successful and fulfilling. Problems often start because we've made sex seem like such a focal point of a good relationship and we've come to believe that without instant sexual attraction, there can't ever be a satisfying, happy relationship.

That is just not true. Women in arranged marriages prove it. Modern sexual history is overflowing with stories of women trying to have relationships with men they've had great sex with, but with whom they share pretty much nothing else in common. I don't know if you've ever been there but I certainly have, and nothing brings this point home better than struggling through the awkwardness and boredom of trying to turn a few good nights into something more.

But instead of my story, I'm going to tell you about a very similar experience that Leena, a close friend of mine, had right around the same time as my debacle. Leena is 32 and the owner of an accessories store in the Washington, D.C., area. Her experience with trying to make sex into something more led her to heartbreak and frustration.

"John and I met walking our dogs in my local park. John is really fit, with dark hair and green eyes, and I just instantly felt drawn to him." Leena and John started hanging out together, and this quickly led to sex. "I just always wanted to be near him or touching him. The sex was amazing! I was convinced that I'd found my soul mate, since I'd never been this physically into anyone else before."

Unfortunately, apart from the sex, Leena started to realize that she and John didn't actually get along that well. "I'm pretty committed to certain political causes and John would always put them down and make comments about me being a 'left-wing granola cruncher,' which hurt."

Leena soon realized she hated John's political views, and lack of interest in culture or people different from him. "I was so stupid, but I just couldn't believe that we could be having amazing sex and this powerful chemistry and that there wasn't something bigger about us being together."

Determined to find a deeper connection, Leslie tried involving him in her work with developing countries, suggesting that they make travel plans to Asia or South Africa. "Finally, after seven months together, I started to realize that I actually didn't like or respect John, and just as I was getting it together to end it, he told me that he'd started sleeping with a waitress at our local bar. So at least he made it easy for me."

Good sex is simply not enough to keep a couple together long-term. We just spend too much of our day-to-day lives out of bed! As Leslie found out, your marriage musts are infinitely more important.

So what is the right role for sex in a relationship, and how can you build—and, more importantly, maintain—sexual chemistry over time? Women in arranged marriages have some very specific answers for us.

The Arranged-Marriage Way

No matter how open you might be to the idea that arranged marriage has lessons to teach us about relationships, I can understand if the idea of sex advice from arranged marriages might seem like something of a reach! Or, like some of my friends, you might be wondering if women in arranged marriages are trained experts in the exotic secrets of the Kama Sutra. Sorry, but no—you'll have to read a different book for that.

Based on all my interviews, observations, and conversations, when it comes to the arranged-marriage approach to sex, there are three main lessons that any woman can apply to her life, no matter where she is or what's going on in her relationships right now. You'll recognize some of these themes from the stories we've already discussed, but we'll talk about them in greater detail now.

1. **A man's attractiveness is largely based on your feelings about yourself.** In earlier chapters we've explored the fact that women in arranged marriages don't expect their husbands to fulfill their every need; this chapter's stories have shown how this theory extends to attraction and sex. While I'm not suggesting that you could be attracted to any man on Earth, I am suggesting that when your marriage musts are evident, sexual attraction can and does grow.

2. **Sex is best when it's put into perspective.** Women in arranged marriages treat sex as one element of their relationships. It is no more important a factor than any other aspect of their compatibility or satisfaction with a partner.

3. **The best way to have good sex and maintain sexual attraction is to focus on the positives in your partner.** Quite simply, what you put your attention on expands in your mind, so the more you focus on what is attractive about your partner, the more you will be attracted to him.

Let's first look at the basics of sex in arranged marriages. Since the couple may or may not have ever met before the wedding, sex initially has no direct role. (In the age of cell phones and text messages, however, a few of the younger couples that I spoke with admitted to organizing surreptitious meetings after the engagement or during the wedding planning process!)

That's not to say that there isn't a definite overtone of sex, especially with the rituals and traditions around traditional arranged-marriage weddings, many of which are focused on getting the bride ready for her new life and role. But what I learned from my interviews is that, just as it's a myth to think that women in arranged marriages must be in loveless marriages, it's equally a myth to think that women in arranged marriages don't have satisfying, fulfilling sex lives. Do all of them? No, of course not. But then, that's hardly something unique to women in arranged marriages!

During my interviews I heard about a range of sexual experiences, from one couple where the wife introduced the desire for a threesome, to another, where, as a result of some medical problems, the couple still has not had sex after five years of marriage. Among the older arranged-marriage couples that I spoke with, it was common for neither of the partners to have had any sexual experience prior to their marriage.

Usha, 68, is the grandmother of three and has been married for almost forty-three years; she is an active volunteer and an accomplished cook. Every time I went over to talk to her, she fed me the most amazing homemade meat and vegetable samosas. To my surprise, talking about sex with Usha wasn't nearly as awkward as I thought it would be, particularly since she seemed to genuinely relish a chance to recall the early days of her marriage.

"About a week before the wedding, my youngest masi [an Indian term for the aunt on the mother's side] took me shopping for jewelry and just started telling me about her wedding night and what to expect." She laughs, "I'd heard stories from girls at school, but to be honest, I couldn't picture anything like that happening; I'd never even been allowed to be alone with a boy before, not even a male cousin! But I wasn't scared; nervous yes, but excited to finally be seen as an adult! About a year after our wedding, my husband told me that he was embarrassed that he seemed so frightened and nervous on our wedding night compared to me!"

From the Man's Point of View . . .

While my interviews covered a broad age, geographic, and social range, there is one group that is clearly not represented here: the husbands. Along the way, I had numerous offers from husbands in arranged marriages who were keen to be interviewed, and a few who felt that without speaking to them, I wasn't actually getting a complete picture. They are right. But when I started doing these interviews, I didn't actually have this or any book in mind and it was the women's stories that I identified with and was curious about.

Although I didn't do complete interviews with the man in arranged marriages, I did ask a few of them for their general thoughts and experiences on their relationships, just to get a taste of their side of their story.

"I came to the United States to go the college and had a girlfriend here, but I ended it when we graduated because I knew my family would never accept her. And even though she didn't want to admit it, her family probably wouldn't have accepted me. Things were like that then. I met my wife once before we got married. I remember thinking that she was very pretty but seemed shy. But after thirty-two years together, I would say it's been good, and I think for the most part, we've both been happy."

—Anil, 61

"I'm the only one of my friends who had an arranged marriage. I never really thought I would, but suddenly I was forty, I was working too much to date, and I didn't want to go through all the games with someone. The biggest surprise for me is that along the way I actually met so many women who sounded like people I would like to date—nothing like the image people have. It's funny, people think arranged marriages are so 'exotic,' but what most of them don't know is that they probably have a least a couple of colleagues or friends who have had one. My wife is amazing; my family met her family first and then we all met. She works in development and has lived all over. It's been a wonderful three years so far."

—Sanjay, 45

"My wife was quite young when we got married. Not just in age—she was nineteen and I was twenty-five—but in experience. There were a lot of adjustments at first since she had never lived away from home before and had a hard time figuring things out when we moved to the United States. I did my best to be patient and helped her a lot. In some ways it was a tough time, but in some ways I think it helped bring us closer. We still laugh about some of the things that happened then."

—Saiyad, 57

"We didn't meet until after the wedding, and I was so nervous. It's funny no one ever thinks that the man might be nervous also. I really wanted my wife to like me. It's been sixteen years now, and we have three kids. We've had our problems and we fight, but I feel very lucky to have her."

—Arun, 52

For younger and North American–born couples, the arranged-marriage sex stories tended to be quite different. Reena is a 37-year-old journalist in Canada, who is married with three kids. She had two fairly serious relationships before deciding to have an arranged marriage.

"A few days after our engagement had been decided, my husband and I started to call each other, and during one of these conversations, I told him about my past relationships. It was something I know neither of our parents would have done or probably have had to do, but it was important to us. Hamish had grown up here as well, and at the time of our engagement he was thirty-eight, so just as I had suspected, he had a bit of history behind him as well!"

Everything You Always Wanted to Know About Sex in Arranged Marriages (Well, Sort Of)

Finally, the part we've all been waiting for! As you know, I've had a lifelong fascination with arranged marriages, and I admit that much of my curiosity and many of my questions centered around the whole issue of sex. As you can probably imagine, the questions about sex were some of the most difficult ones for me to bring up in my interviews, but since my curiosity was much stronger than any feelings of embarrassment, I pushed on.

Here are a few of the questions I asked. They may have perhaps crossed your mind also while reading this book.

- What is it really like to start having sex with a person who is essentially a stranger?
- How do you build attraction?
- Can the sex be really, really hot?
- What do you do if it isn't?

Since I had no real context for what sex in an arranged marriage was like (I'm sure you understand that I never asked my parents about their sex life when I was growing up!), I hypothesized that it must be a bit like a casual pickup or one-night stand. Except that in this case someone else did the picking up for you, and instead of nicely leaving in the early hours of the morning, the guy stayed forever to share your bathroom. Hmmmm.

I was more wrong than I could possibly imagine. And I am grateful to my interviewees for being amazingly open about their most intimate experiences and sharing their stories and insights with me.

The First Time

When it comes to initial feelings of sexual attraction among arranged-marriage couples, the experiences were across the board. Some described a surprising sense of comfort. Others were quite instantly attracted to their husbands when they first saw them—and going through some of the wedding albums I could see why!

The other aspect that I hadn't realized was that contrary to what I'd always thought, many couples in arranged marriages actually waited quite a while after the wedding before they started to have sex. Honeymoon periods were literally the time that they got to know each other. Couples who were still in school or headed overseas said they waited anywhere from three weeks to five months to have sex for the first time.

In the Bedroom

———◦◦◦◦———

Let's face it: first time sex is generally awkward. Away from the movies, how can it not be? There's just so much room for things to go wrong, and even if it is enjoyable, there's still an element of nervousness. And that's when you're dating! So what's it like in an arranged marriage? The experiences were varied, but read on for a quick sneak peak:

- "I was so nervous about what would happen on the wedding night, but after all that hype, *nothing* happened! We were both too nervous. We ended up waiting almost a month."

- "I can't say I liked it at first, but I was keen to tell my sisters about it."

- "I felt very comfortable, not relaxed, but comfortable."

- "He seemed so happy that I was surprised! It got better as the first year went on."

- "I loved it. I thought my husband was so handsome. It was wonderful."

- "I wasn't keen on it at all! So we stopped and once we were more used to each other, it got better."

- "A new person is always a bit funny for me, and this time I was married but I didn't know him. I just knew lots about him. I felt like at first it wasn't really us—what I mean is not the us that it is now."

Why It Works: "Like a Cold Pot That Gradually Comes to a Boil"

The sexual pattern of arranged marriages is essentially the reverse of couples in love matches. Most love matches start relationships on a sexual high; there's incredible attraction and chemistry and all you want to do is tuck yourselves away from the rest of the world to be alone together. As time goes on and the relationship evolves and matures, this feeling gradually starts to wear down and dissipate.

Arranged marriages, on the other hand, often start out quite neutrally, but as the couple becomes increasingly intimate over time, the attraction and enjoyment also increase. Anu, a 58-year-old pharmacist, mother of three girls, and close family friend, used an analogy that really stuck in my mind. According to her, the difference is that a love marriage is like a boiling pot that cools down over time, while an arranged marriage is like a cold pot that gradually comes to a boil.

Shameem, 43, is a junior high English teacher with two kids. She had an arranged marriage when she was 24 and agrees that, for her, sex with her husband is far more enjoyable now than when they were first married. Her husband, Rishi, was 28 when they were married at a lavish wedding in New Jersey.

"Rishi was the son of one of my parents' close friends," says Shameem, "so I knew of him for years, but didn't really know him. We'd probably spoken no more than twice in our lives. Even after our engagement we didn't really see each other or talk, so after the wedding it was like suddenly being alone with someone you'd seen around but never spoken to. And we were both so nervous!

"It took us a while before we started having sex; I can't remember now, but maybe six or eight weeks or actually maybe even more, and I don't remember being that excited by it," Shameem laughs. "For me, it changed when our son Vikram was born. I felt more confident about myself and so much closer to Rishi. Now that the kids are getting more independent and we have a bit more time alone, it's quite exciting!"

Notice how Shameem had the best sex when she felt best about herself and her circumstances. And because she never had high expectations of hot, steamy movie sex with her husband, Shameem's excitement is even more special and joyful.

Why It Works: Putting Sex in Perspective

Now let's focus in on the second success factor regarding sexual satisfaction in arranged marriages: perspective. Women in arranged marriages view their relationships holistically. Because they clearly see their marriages as being the result of, and built on, so many other factors, sex doesn't assume the front-and-center starring role in the relationship.

Mehri, a 43-year-old product manager, met her husband Harry just once (and with both sets of parents and a grandparent each in tow!) before they got engaged. "I had dated and had serious relationships before I was married, so when I decided to go down the arranged-marriage route, all my friends thought I was crazy! And of course the whole sex thing was one of the biggest issues.

"Even after the engagement, since we lived at opposite ends of the country, we didn't meet up again until the week of the wedding—and everything was so crazy then that it was really not until we flew out to Jamaica for our honeymoon that we actually got a chance to really be alone. Harry is nice-looking, not what I'd describe as my type, but attractive enough." Of course we now know this doesn't matter all that much!

"You know, it's funny, but I really don't find our sex life all that different than most of my friends or even my past relationships. I've been married for five years and we have two daughters, and, you know, it's nice when we have it, but lots of times, we're just too tired. The difference is that I don't stress about it as much as my other friends."

The sense that I got from the interviews with women like Mehri was that sex was a part of marriage, but it was just one element among so many others. Despite being surrounded by media and women's magazine messages that couples need to constantly work on their sex lives, women in arranged marriages just don't obsess about their sex lives. Maybe because sex wasn't what brought them together with their mates, it had less power to pull them apart.

Hanina, 41, is an accountant at one of the big firms in London and has been married for seven years. She and her arranged-marriage husband, Harry, recently had their third daughter. "I'll admit that sex with Harry [a man she saw a picture of but never met before marrying] is not the hottest, but you know what, it's still the happiest relationship I've ever had. And it doesn't seem to matter that much. I know it's not why we got together in the first place, so to be honest it doesn't worry me the way it might have if we'd dated before."

It was a theme I heard echoed often: maybe sex in an arranged marriage wasn't the most exciting thing, but it was good and one small part of a much more complex and meaningful relationship. As Anya, a 35-year-old marketing manager, explained to me, "When I was dating, I'll be honest, I had a lot of so-so, not-sure-why-I-bothered sex, I-just-had-too-much-to-drink sex. This isn't like that at all because my husband is such a sweet man and what we are building and doing together is so much bigger."

Usha, the excellent cook I mentioned earlier, best described the importance of putting sex in perspective. "It's important, yes, but being intimate in other ways is more important. When you are young you might not think so, or you might think that a marriage based on friendship, family, shared years, and the sense that you can rely on someone is boring or just settling, but that will change. As you get older, you realize that there is no greater blessing than having had a genuine partner for so many years."

When it comes to building a sex life with an essential stranger, women in arranged marriages take what can only be called a practical approach: they really and truly focus on the positives of their partners. When I first started to notice this trend, I disdained it, thinking that there was something false and Pollyanna-ish about it.

But five years ago, when I first started putting the word out that I was looking for women in arranged marriages to interview, the first set of people who volunteered were from my parents' circle of friends, relatives, and acquaintances. This meant that, with the initial fifty to sixty interviews, the husbands were often men I knew or had at least met. And so, I was particularly surprised at some of the descriptions and views that their wives had of them—since it was quite different from how I saw them. (Which, of course, shows that an outsider never knows the truth about a couple's intimate relations!)

And yet, I still wondered if they were sugarcoating their relationships for me. It wasn't that these women didn't have any complaints or frustrated comments (who doesn't?), but overall, they seemed incredibly focused on what they saw as their husband's positive characteristics and qualities. And this pattern continued even as my interview pool expanded across ethnicities, countries, age groups, and socioeconomic differences. I gradually realized that this approach of focusing on your partner's positives just makes sense—particularly when you're in a relationship with someone you are effectively just getting to know, but with whom you want to make it work. After all, if you're already married (and want to stay that way), what's the point of focusing on anything other than the positives?

And the thing is, their approach really works! What you focus on really does become what you believe. What you focus on, whether it's a person or a situation, changes how you think, feel, and act. So when entering into an arranged marriage, it makes sense to focus on the positive qualities and traits of this person that you didn't really know, but that you believed was a decent person and that you were determined to make a life with. This positive focus and approach would naturally start creating feelings of warmth and appreciation between the two of you—much more so than thinking about what it was that you felt was missing or wished were different. (Please note that in no way does this theory apply to a relationship with a man who is abusive—mentally, physically, or sexually. If you are in such a situation, please seek support immediately.)

Elaine, a 27-year-old development studies student at the London School of Economics, spoke to me about her initial adjustment with her husband of just ten months. "When we first got married, I wanted to go out to restaurants and shopping so much more than Danny did. I mean, we were both new to London and I wanted to have a bit more fun. But he was always so conscious of what we were spending that it could be really frustrating." But she added soon after that, "He's so focused on saving money to try and get us on the property ladder that I think it's actually quite sweet and it makes me feel really safe."

Why don't we all focus on the positives, like Elaine? Maybe it's from years of dating and hours spent bonding with our girlfriends as we analyze all the possible faults and issues of the newest men in our lives. Most of us are guilty of doing the opposite of Elaine. We focus on the negatives, the things that we wish we could change, thinking about how much better, happier, and more in love we would be "if only." I know I've done it; who hasn't? But the results are never what we want.

This tendency to try to change our men instead of our own focus really struck me when I went to lunch recently with one of my cousins and several of her friends. All six of them were newlyweds in arranged marriages. As I expected, the table conversation quickly turned to men, relationships, and their new husbands and marriages. (Yes, women in arranged marriages still spend hours gossiping about their relationships!) At first, I couldn't figure out what seemed so different about a situation that seemed so normal—a group of fashionably dressed women, drinking white wine spritzers, ordering salads but eating the group fries while they laughed and gossiped about their new partners.

What made their conversation different? Yes, there was the arranged-marriage factor—that they hadn't known their husbands before marrying—but it wasn't just that. What surprised me was that the nature of their conversation seemed so positive compared to what I was used to. When I get together with my girlfriends who were not in arranged relationships, it seems that too often after the first glass of wine, we all start complaining about the men in our lives and what we want to change or fix about them.

So what does this have to do with sex? Well, I know from personal experience that after a night of complaining about my husband, sex is the last thing I want!

The bottom line: focusing on your partner's positives is crucial to helping build up feelings of attraction and warmth, which are the foundation of a solid and lasting sexual connection.

Hey, a Little Help Doesn't Hurt!

———— ✧ ————

I am willing to admit that sometimes a man's sexual prowess might need a little help—but I guarantee you this is not unique to either arranged marriages or love matches! So, here is my unscientific advice: pick up any lifestyle magazine in any month and read—and share!—some articles on improving your sex life, making your marriage hot, or tricks to get him interested.

Hot sex and good sex are clearly important in a relationship. I would never tell you otherwise. . . .

Okay, so what do the three elements of sexual attraction in arranged marriages—knowing the role of your feelings about yourself, putting sex in perspective, and focusing on the positives—mean for you?

Above all, this chapter has shown that despite what most of us believe, sexual attraction is not just something that passively happens to you, but it is something that you can influence. I'm not saying that you need to start dating guys you aren't remotely attracted to, but you will benefit greatly from a slight shift in your views on sex and sexual attraction. In practical terms, it means you should start by making sure you focus on you! Regularly indulge in the self-love exercise in this chapter. The more you feel sexy, confident, and happy, the more you will have sexual attraction in your life—possibly with a man you never expected!

Also remember that sex is only one factor in a happy, healthy relationship. Let's face it, odds are that regardless of what I say, how good your intentions are or how determined you are to get into a happy long-term relationship, you might be tempted by some hot guy who comes your way. If the hottie meets your marriage musts and wants a relationship, then lucky you! If he doesn't, then be careful. Remember that when we first meet someone whom we're superattracted to, we often forget our marriage musts or excuse them. Don't let this happen to you.

Next time you meet a Mr. No Instant Chemistry who *does* meet your marriage musts, even if you don't feel that he's your type, follow the minimum two-date rule. During your dates, keep in mind all the factors under your control that could be affecting how you feel—from the story you are telling yourself about him in your head to where you are directing your attention and focus when you are with him. Instead of thinking about how you aren't attracted to him or how you would be attracted to him "if only," put your attention on what you like about him and for the two dates, act like you are attracted to him. After all, you never know what might happen.

These recommendations apply equally well once you're dating or in a relationship. Focus on the positives in your boyfriend or partner—both sexual and otherwise. Make a list each day of all the things you love about your partner. Compliment him on the things you love. Tell him when he makes you happy. You'll be amazed how these little positive changes can have major effects on your attraction to your man.

And remember to put sex into perspective. Stop focusing on it for a while. Stop counting how often you do—or don't—do it. Stop asking your friends how often they do—or don't—do it. Stop reading statistics in magazines about how often the average couple has sex. In other words, stop talking, thinking, and analyzing it. And of course, *just do it!*

Living This Secret

- **Remember that sex starts with you.** It's how *you* feel that makes the difference between attraction and ambivalence, so whether it's a big date, or a first-time setup, do everything you can to make sure *you're* feeling attractive and positive. Your feelings about a guy—any guy—start with your feelings about yourself. The more positive and attractive you feel, the more attractive you fill find the men you meet.

- **The musts matter more than anything.** Beauty fades. A man who meets your marriage musts will make a much better long-term partner than a man whose best quality is his looks. Just as you wouldn't want a man to love you only for your looks, focus on the deeper qualities of a man. Your definitions of attraction and chemistry will expand in the process.

- **Focus on the positives.** When you make it a point to focus on the positives in a man, whether it's with a man you just met or your partner of the past ten years, you feel more attracted to him. What you put your attention on expands, so put your attention on the things you like!

- **Put sex in perspective.** Although it's hard to believe from the sexually charged culture that surrounds us, sex is only one element of a successful relationship. Of course it's important, but it's only one piece of a larger picture. Don't give sex more power than that!

Chapter Seven

Secret #7

Family Matters

A Higher Purpose = Long-Term Happiness

Melanie is tall and thin and has what I can only describe as expensive-looking blonde hair. She's telling me her views on the whole idea of "opposites attracting," based on her experiences with Erik, an ex-fiancé she recently went out with again. Although both of them are doctors and went to same med school, that's pretty much where the similarity ends. In contrast to Melanie, Erik is shorter and stockier, and he has wild, curly dark hair usually accessorized with either a goatee or a beard.

Shortly before they both turned 33, they decided that after three tumultuous years together they were ready to get married. Sadly, the engagement lasted only ten months before they separated.

"Erik and I had always had our differences, but that had also been part of the excitement and attraction," Melanie says. Melanie grew up and remains very close to her four brothers and parents; "unnaturally so," according to Erik. Melanie's father was the head of a small but highly successful architecture company and her parents own a number of innovative and impressive properties around the country. Her mother divides her time between teaching at a prestigious university and curating exhibits for museums. When Melanie was 11 she went away to boarding school, and although she remembers missing her sisters and her dog, she really enjoyed her time there. "Although Erik often accused me of living in a bubble world where I don't have any idea of real life, I know I was very lucky with my family, especially compared to him."

Erik and his family had immigrated from Mexico when he was 10. Significantly younger than his sisters, who had long since left home, he was often lonely since his parents, both shift workers, were rarely home. Unlike Melanie's almost golden childhood, Erik grew up with frustrated parents, an occasionally violent father, and a sense that life was going to be a struggle. Overweight and quiet, Erik was highly academic and won a full scholarship after high school to Brown University, which he recognized as his avenue to a different life.

"Part of what attracted to me to Erik was that he had already achieved so much and all on his own," Melanie explains. But while Melanie admired him, she now acknowledges that she didn't really understand him. "It took me a year of therapy before I realized that I had always been so focused on what we were doing now or our plans for the future that I never really thought about what it took for him to get here or become this person."

Once they were engaged, their ups and downs took on an entirely new level of stress, particularly as wedding plans and family expectations seemed to exacerbate their differences. "It seemed that after the engagement, small things would somehow become huge fights," Melanie says. "I remember one time I made some comment about how I hated it when he read the paper at the dinner table while we were supposed to be eating together. It just escalated from there into a shouting match. It reached the point where everything we seemed to do or say led to a fight. He accused me of not wanting to see his friends. I felt the same about his feelings about seeing my parents, who had never been anything but welcoming to him. We just had such different views on what day-to-day life should be like, what it meant to be a family together."

Family matters.

It matters when we pick a spouse, it matters in how we understand and relate to that person, it matters in the way we build a long-term relationship, and it matters because, ultimately, family is one of the biggest influencers on a person. And yet, family—and the family we will build together—has increasingly become lower and lower on our list of priorities to consider when we meet someone.

When was the last time you or your friends thought about the type of family your Mr. Right would have? It doesn't really fit with what we usually think about, does it? Often a man's family is an afterthought or a minor plus (if you like his family) or minus (if you don't). Some couples don't even meet each other's parents until months, or even years, into a relationship.

Christina, 32, completely understands this. Born and raised in New Jersey, she's currently living in Paris and working for an American company. Rick, her boyfriend of two years, is from Iowa. Although they've recently started talking about getting engaged, Christina has never met anyone in Rick's family and expects she probably won't until the engagement, possibly even the wedding. "Iowa is not exactly a quick trip or on the top of my list of vacation spots," she points out. "But no, it really doesn't bother me if I don't meet them. The way I see it, I'm marrying Rick, not his family. And I don't think he's that close with them anyway." She adds, "Living in Iowa, it's not like they're going to be involved in my day-to-day life or anything!"

In part, the decline of the role of family in our relationships is the result of modern realities, the ease of travel and a global economy. People no longer live in the same town, state, or even country as their families. Families are fragmented and vacation time is limited, and so, as with Christina, it's not that uncommon to date someone seriously or even become engaged before meeting your partner's family. But this doesn't mean it's a good thing.

Introducing your intended mate to your family does have another side: the feedback. I know that when my parents and aunts met my husband for the first time, they were practically taking notes so they could share their opinions with me! Family feedback may not always be welcome, but often, hidden among the commentary can be genuine insight. While you don't have to accept every comment your family makes, family members often tell us the things that friends frequently won't or don't. Veronica, a 34-year-old journalist and former colleague, has often commented: "If only my family could meet some of my dates a bit early on, I wouldn't keep ending up in bad situations." For the past ten years she's been living in the United Kingdom, while her parents (oil ex-pats) have been stationed essentially across the world in Qatar. Meanwhile, Veronica has had more than her share of dating dramas and disasters, from men who were hiding divorces that haven't been finalized to others who were manipulative and emotionally abusive.

"I wasted two years dealing with the drama of Henry's depression, addiction, and cheating, because I felt that I shouldn't give up on him. I followed him up with David, who ended up inviting me to move in essentially so I could pay all of his bills. I've often felt that if my family had been able to meet them earlier, I wouldn't have gotten so involved since they would have seen the signs I was missing or too infatuated to see." At the same time, she continues, "I've often thought that if the men I was dating were able to casually meet my family, then they would have a better idea of who I was and why I did or said certain things."

Logistics aside, many of us have an instinctive issue with the idea that someone's family should be a factor in a relationship. Perhaps because this scares us or makes us feel dependent, we discount the influence and importance that family actually has both on a person and on a relationship.

Many of us could probably relate to Katherine's feelings: "Even though I now see how the differences in our families was the source of a great deal of our tension, I still feel uncomfortable with the idea that someone's family should matter if you love him."

Katherine's view is completely understandable. Family is something that a person can't control or change, so it just seems wrong to judge a potential partner based on his family. Plus, it's uncomfortable to think that a man would decide to marry or not marry us based on our families. Not to mention that it seems to go against the best of American ideals: you shouldn't be judged on where you came from but on what you do and become.

All of these feelings are reasonable and legitimate. But here's the thing: There's a difference between appreciating and understanding the influence and importance that family (whether directly or indirectly) has on a relationship and actually holding someone's background against him. My point of view is that family needs to be a serious consideration in your choice of a life partner.

Fairly factoring family into our relationship equation is often made quite difficult by the fact that many of us are in denial about how influenced we actually are by our own family backgrounds.

"I had never really given any thought to how my family had influenced me, and to be honest, just went with the assumption that I was who I was because I wanted to be," says 34-year-old Emily, a policy adviser for the city government in Toronto. This view of herself and her family shifted dramatically after the birth of her first child, two years ago. To her surprise, she suddenly found herself increasingly frustrated with her husband, Phil. "I grew up in a house with two teachers, and my parents were all about reading, learning, and education. I really enjoyed school and want those same things for my daughter Anya."

Unlike Emily, Phil happily left formal education after high school, but had done really well financially with three industrial-parts stores. "I'm really proud of what Phil's accomplished, but I can't stand it when he talks about how he's made all this money without going to college. I don't want Anya growing up listening to his views and opinions. I want her to go to college." Emily admits that she doesn't know what she'll do about a situation that has taken her fully by surprise. "I was genuinely shocked to find myself sounding just like my mother talking about the importance of going to a good college! I never realized how much I'd actually taken from my parents' thinking before."

Regardless of whether a person is estranged from or very close to his family, understanding a potential partner's family background will provide insight into many of his actions and decisions, both positive and negative, as well as reactive and proactive. This is what 29-year-old Jean found when she and Ryan, her boyfriend of almost a year, ran into some severe financial problems. At the time, they were both graduate students in Texas. Ryan's student funding hadn't come through and Jean had just lost out on a teaching job she'd been counting on. Both were in debt. "To make matters worse, we'd gone completely over budget doing up our apartment together, largely because Ryan kept insisting that we should buy better and better stuff." Financial problems are tough on any couple, but what made it more difficult for Jean is that, "I just couldn't understand why Ryan would always put such a positive spin on our situation when we were in real trouble. To be honest, it just made me crazy to listen to him."

At that time, Jean had never met Ryan's family and only knew superficial details about them. "I knew that his dad had had some financial problems, but that was it." That Thanksgiving, she went to Ryan's parents' house in Maine for the first time, even though it was almost ten months later. "It was like a lightbulb going off for me. Suddenly I had a whole new understanding of Ryan and why something like getting a new couch instead of a used one mattered to him so much. The house and furniture were really run down and it was clear that finances were a bit of struggle. I could see how Ryan just wanted to distance himself from it."

Since an increasing number of us live farther away from our families and see them less and less, there is a tendency to feel that they are separate from our personal or relationship lives. While this may be true in terms of daily contact or interactions, our families still influence so much of who we are, what we believe (whether agreeing or disagreeing with what we grew up with), and what we want for our futures. Think about your own family and answer the following questions:

- What values are most important to your family? Education? Faith? Helping others less fortunate? Making money? Being healthy? Loyalty? Culture?

- In what ways do you want your future family (your husband and children, if you want to have them) to resemble the family in which you grew up?

- In what ways do you want your future family to be different?

- Are there any family values that would be unacceptable for a potential partner to have?

- How much time did your family spend together? What was it like? What did you do? What are some favorite memories?

The Arranged-Marriage Way:
Family Is the Starting Point of Marriage

It would be an understatement to say that family matters in an arranged marriage! In arranged marriages, family is seen as being one of the most important factors when thinking about a possible candidate for marriage. In arranged-marriage culture, a person's family is seen as the best predictor of a person's character, behavior, and future life.

This focus on family also comes from the fact that traditionally (although it is still quite common today) brides would live with their husband's family. Since your daughter would be living with this new family, making sure she would fit in, be happy, and be well treated was understandably an essential concern.

With an arranged marriage, asking, "What is the family like?" doesn't just mean top-line details of the parents or siblings. "The family" can easily include questions about parents, grandparents, siblings, in-laws, first cousins, aunts, uncles, great uncles, great aunts, their children—you get the idea!

Similarly, the innocuous-seeming phrase of "What are they like?" means, "Tell me everyone's professional and educational background (including high school and elementary school), where everyone is living, whether they are "well settled" (meaning who they have married, what they do, who their family is), any vices or scandals you may have heard about, who their friends are (and of course what they do), some thumbnail sketches on personality, whether they are "good to their family" (do they help each other out? what have they done?), any health problems you might have heard about, community involvement or honors they may have, and finally, some third-party names that can substantiate and verify all of the above. All together, it's serious due diligence!

Mrs. Bennet Would Approve

One of the funnier things that I heard about during my interviews was what families did to get ready before they stepped into the arranged-marriage fray. In order to get the best match for their sons or daughters, they had to present themselves and their families in the best way they could. The result?

The women I spoke with told me about house renovations being done a year before they were going to start seeing families, new furniture being bought (and, in one case, returned in between meetings), and of course new clothes for everyone involved. I also heard about more attractive single cousins and sisters being told to be conveniently absent on the day of the match, trophies and academic awards being moved so they would be easily spotted, and in one case, a man parking his friend's Mercedes outside the house in hopes that the girl's family would just assume it was his.

Before the Internet, due diligence on a potential partner's family involved many letters, carefully planned long-distance calls, and lengthy meetings over tea. One woman I spoke with told me how her family spent three years researching people, during which time two of the people they were considering married other people. She said she was worried that she would be too old to get married by the time they agreed on someone!

Investigating and providing references for families in the marriage market has been the life's work of several of my great-aunts who spend their days sipping tea in various drawing rooms and clubs as they help arrange various marriages by providing details on one family while asking questions of another. More recently, when one of my cousins was in the process of having his marriage arranged, my grandmother was adamant that my father (then living in Dallas) be on hand in Delhi to "meet" the prospective families of the girls being considered and answer questions about ours.

While this is the traditional way of doing things, methods are being adapted to reflect the changes in arranged marriages over time. As we've talked about, in the past, parents or relatives searched their own social networks for suitable prospects for their children. Today, however, they often look online (India's biggest matrimonial portal, Shaadi.com, has 9.1 million users and the site reports 720,000 marriages started by them), even though the prospect of anonymity could lead to fraud. The issue has been resolved by the rise in premarital investigations.

The investigations are usually taken when the match is almost finalized and usually take about a week to ten days. The idea is to confirm or provide details about the type of information that can no longer be confirmed through family and friendship networks. This includes details about previous and present relationships, education, career, and financial position. The extended family is checked out also. "The numbers [using a detective before marriage] have almost doubled in the last two years," says Sanjay Singh, CEO of the New Delhi–based Indian Detective Agency. "Earlier it was just high-profile and very rich families that were engaging services. But now it's mostly the middle classes."

Another slightly off-beat example of just how important family is in arranged marriage was recently reported by Reuters. Apparently, villagers at a wedding in eastern India had decided that the intended groom arrived too drunk to get married, so at the invitation of the bride's family, the groom's younger brother took his place instead!

In arranged marriages, family is so important that the process can make the individual feel secondary to his or her relatives. That's what happened when 33-year-old Shayna from San Francisco was having her marriage arranged. A strategy consultant turned hatha yoga teacher, she admits that, at times, the focus on her family almost made her change her mind about the whole arranged-marriage plan. "I had no problem with all the questions and digging about me; that all made sense and was really one of the reasons that I'd decided to have an arranged marriage." But all the questions about her extended family started to get to her. "I knew that my family was probably doing the same thing, but that didn't help. I just kept thinking that usually the bride is the complete center of attention and here we are talking about my sister's education and my brother-in-law's job!" Unfortunately for Shayna, my interviews suggest that the tradition of extensive family research won't be ending anytime soon. It is fundamental to the entire philosophy of why arranged marriages are successful.

Ankita, a 58-year-old mother of two in Cleveland, had not only had an arranged marriage, but as she proudly tells me, has also been instrumental in arranging four other marriages. A recent widow (her husband passed away last year) she was married for 39 years. "They were good years," she tells me over dim sum and green tea one winter afternoon. "I miss talking to Arun every day, and every morning it's like a fresh shock realizing he's not here anymore."

Describing their marriage, she says it was the perfect example of what her mother always said an arranged marriage should be: "the bringing together of two people from similar backgrounds, but with opposite natures." When I ask her to explain, she laughs. "Arun was relaxed, easygoing, and so patient; he never seemed to get angry or irritated." She smiles at the memory. "Me, I'm the opposite: hot tempered, short-tempered, and always rushing around. We balanced each other out."

Arun and Aasha were married when she was 19 and he was 25. "We didn't see each other until the wedding, and then I was so nervous that I don't think I was able to look him in the face for almost a month into our marriage!" Before her wedding, Aasha's mother had told her not to worry or be too nervous, saying that she would soon feel comfortable with him because "his family is just like ours." This was particularly important in Aasha's case, since for the first five years of their relationship, she lived with her in-laws.

"She was right; Arun and I seemed to both understand where the other was coming from and his family home was so much like ours that I didn't find it that difficult to adjust at all."

Family Is Also About the Future

While family background is a key factor in an arranged marriage, actually *having* a family is equally important. It is very rare that couples in arranged marriages make a conscious decision not to have children. Among the women I spoke with, there were several who didn't have kids, but in such cases that had been the result of circumstances rather than planning. In part, this focus on starting a family is the result of the traditional nature of arranged marriages, where children are seen as the center of family and married life.

In fact, as 28-year-old Indra found, the pressure to start having a family can be immediate. Married for a just a year, she and her 31-year-old husband, Neil, moved to California shortly after their wedding in Mumbai, India. Bubbly and friendly, Indra is keen to work on building her career in advertising before starting a family. Her husband agrees with this idea, particularly since he wants them to be able to travel and get to know each other a bit. (They were actually one of the few younger couples I spoke with who didn't even speak or e-mail before the wedding.) "We both want a family, of course, but in a couple of years. But try telling that to either of our parents! I feel like since the wedding, they've just been dropping hints, asking questions, and watching my waistline—which has grown, but not for the reasons they're hoping!"

Why It Works

This focus on family shouldn't be confused with the idea that arranged marriages depend on actually *liking* the family. (In that case, hardly anyone would be getting married!) No, what is considered to be a "suitable" or "good" family to make a match with is one that shares the same basic values, customs, and beliefs as your family.

This approach is based on the belief that bringing together people with similar family backgrounds will:

1. Increase the chance that they will understand where the other person is coming from on both big decisions and the small habits and quirks of everyday married life.

2. Increase the chance that they will share common values and views, which as we saw earlier, is an essential factor to the success of arranged marriages.

Munira, 36, is a travel agent and mother of three. Married for nine years, she had never really understood the emphasis that arranged marriages placed on finding someone with a similar family background until she and her husband, Ameet, started their family. "When my parents were arranging my marriage, they were adamant about finding someone who had a family like ours—which I guess meant pretty liberal on most things, not overly religious, professional parents, and a strong family life. When Ameet and I had our first daughter, I realized why they were so keen on this point. He and I seemed to have a real agreement about how we should do things with and for our family, an understanding that I think was the result of our similar family experiences."

A Bond for Life

One of the reasons that having children is considered to be so essential in an arranged marriage is that children are seen as a way to bond the couple, to help them give a sense of planning for the future together. And, even more important, children give them a sense of shared purpose that is larger than the two of them. Of course there are other ways to do this, but in an arranged marriage, this is considered the best and easiest way.

Mona is a documentary filmmaker who has been all over Africa and Asia with her work. It was an exciting but disruptive life that made sustaining a relationship difficult. "To be honest, I never had a serious relationship before I was married and I was thirty-eight before I decided to have an arranged marriage. Thirty-eight is on the older side for a love marriage, but it's ancient for an arranged marriage!"

Her husband Deepak was 45 and a widower when they married. "My parents—well, especially my mother—were really worried that I would find the realities of day-to-day marriage difficult. I mean, part of the idea of arranged marriages is to bring people together when they are young so they are adaptable and can grow together, not be already stuck in their ways!" Mona admits that, at first, married life was difficult for her. "I felt like I didn't know how to share my goals, or even my day, with someone else." After a year and a half of marriage, and at the encouragement of her mother, Deepak and Mona decided to adopt two three-year-old sisters from India. "Keloni and Klare are amazing, and bringing them into our life really changed our relationship. They've brought us together and really made us into both a couple and a family."

What This Means for You

Since researching the family of the cute guy you just spoke to at Starbucks would be a little crazy (although you can do amazing things with Google and Facebook these days!), what does all of this mean for you? And what if you specifically don't want someone with the same family background as you?

Ultimately, what arranged marriages show is that family background really matters in terms of how a couple navigates the course of their relationship and life together. It is very important to include a person's family background and upbringing as a factor in your choice of a marriage partner. It is not the single most important factor, but it should be among the factors you consider. The reason is because a person's family background, for better or worse, has an effect on his or her values and the way that person sees the world.

If the idea of finding someone with a similar or complementary family background to yours can seem archaic (or even unappealing), then at least decide to learn about that person's family background so you understand how it might affect your relationship and future together. No matter what you might believe about a particular guy, his family—and what they say, how they act, and where they live—will play a role in your relationship. You may not feel a direct effect, but there is no doubt that a person's flesh-and-blood relations are part of their makeup. This is true even if a partner's parents have passed away. Family is that fundamental to who we are.

How can you find out about a potential partner's family and how his background may affect your relationship?

- If you can't meet them, then ask questions and show interest! The more you know about your potential mate, his childhood, and his home life, the better your understanding of him and your relationship will be.

- Pay attention to clues. How does he talk about his sister? What's his relationship with his parents like? How often does he call his grandmother? Does he have family photos on display in his home?

- What stories does he tell about growing up? Are they mostly positive or negative?

All of the above will provide you with clues as to how a man will be as a member of the family the two of you will create together. Even if your potential partner doesn't much like his family, you can learn if he has some fond memories and fundamental respect. If it sounds like he comes from a very dysfunctional, difficult family, then see if he has addressed this in his life—through finding an alternate family of longtime friends, therapy, or in some other meaningful way.

How can you increase your chances of meeting a man with a family whose values are similar to yours? Well, the marriage musts help, since they help you become clear on what those values actually are. In arranged marriages, the view is very much focused on the idea of finding families that you know, which explains the focus on family friends or matches with people whom a sibling or cousin may know socially or from school. The same can apply to you; look for potential dates within your networks and those of your family and friends.

Much of my advice in this chapter is based on the fact that a married couple is not an island. Any couple is also part of two family units as well as a larger community of friends, colleagues, and neighbors. As romantic as it is to think of "just the two of us," it's not a realistic way to think about your future with a partner. Again, this shows the damage of a "soul mate" or "the one" mentality, which implies that no one and nothing else matters. The reality is that as two, three, fifteen, twenty-five years go by, no matter what intensity you might feel about your mate at the beginning, something more is usually needed to help bring you together as a couple.

Even at the beginning of a relationship, a unifying sense of purpose helps. For instance, as more and more of us are marrying later and working longer, it is easy for couples to eventually drift into parallel or separate lives. The decline in organized religion, common communities, and geographical permanence often further compound feelings of being together but alone.

In arranged marriages, couples are naturally more community- and family-centered because the marriage is part of a larger plan and belief system Nevertheless, the pressure to have a family comes from a desire to bring the couple together over a shared goal or purpose. As we've discussed, usually this means children.

For our purposes of applying arranged marriage theories to *your* life, this same sense of shared purpose could come from any number of goals or dreams. The only real criterion is that it brings the two of you together with sense of doing something for a higher purpose. A common cause or a shared dedication to a goal can infuse a relationship with vitality and purpose. If it's dynamic enough to both of you, it can becomes the active focus that drives a relationship forward and guides it through difficult times.

This shared purpose can provide excitement and energy as well as a sense of perspective. When two people are focused on the achievement of a shared goal or passion for a shared cause, other issues and annoyances that may create conflict dwindle in significance. For some couples this might be religious belief, for others it's a desire to travel the world helping the poor; for some couples it may be a passion for running a business together or raising organic crops on a farm.

Rachel, a 33-year-old litigation lawyer from New York, recently celebrated her sixth wedding anniversary, but she talks about how a year and a half in, being married felt like it was becoming harder and harder. "It seemed like the wedding excitement had worn off and so had the thrill of living together. I was working all the time and felt like I only saw Dan on our date nights, when the pressure of making up for all the nights we hadn't been together would somehow lead to fights." When Dan's mother was diagnosed with breast cancer, both of them resolved to do everything they could to help not just her but also others like her. This year is the fourth year that they're running a marathon to raise money for breast cancer. "We fund-raise together, got involved in the organization and train together. Although this mission came out of a scary event, it definitely brought us closer."

Ultimately, regardless of the what, it's the creation and sharing of a dream, passion, or mission and working together toward achieving it that makes the couple closer and provides the sustaining vision that focuses them. Several couples I spoke with described how having to overcome a financial setback or struggle, dealing with a health scare, or building a business or relocating had given them a greater sense of connection or partnership. Of course the shared goal of raising a family together fits this description perfectly.

I know that my husband, Rana, and I have definitely found that the birth of our son brought an unexpected sense of partnership and joint purpose into our relationship. What we were doing on a day-to-day basis was now about more than just ourselves, it was about taking care of our son Seth, planning for him and making sure that we were working together to make his future what we wanted. The daily work required meant that smaller annoyances or trivial issues were pushed aside and we had a completely different sense of perspective. There has also been something incredibly unexpected and wonderful about seeing an entirely different side of Rana and watching how he relates to our son.

Living This Secret

- **Acknowledge the importance of family history.** A potential partner's family should be a factor in your consideration of that person as a life partner. Whether we like it or not, all of us are affected by the circumstances and values of our relatives.

- **Increase your chances of meeting a family-friendly mate.** Let people close to you know that you are looking for love; you never know who they might turn up with!

- **Make sure your relationship has a larger shared purpose.** Whether it's raising a family together, sharing a deep religious conviction, working toward a cause, or anything else that is meaningful to you, a marriage needs a deeper purpose to keep it together over the long haul.

Conclusion

. . . Then Comes Love

When I started these interviews in 2000, it was out of interest and to learn more about a topic that I had grown up close to but didn't really understand. There was a disconnect between what I thought about arranged marriages (so old-fashioned!) and what I saw in the arranged-marriage couples I knew. Distilling out the seven secrets in this book has been a way for me to bring the two together and find real answers in the experiences of the women I spoke with. I don't know what your views on arranged marriages were before you picked this up or whether they've changed after reading this, but I do hope the lessons I've shared have brought you inspiration and new strategies to try.

While in some ways the arranged-marriage approach to relationships seems completely opposite from ours, with the growth in dating agencies and Internet dating, it seems that there may be more overlap than anyone ever considered. While the practice of arranged marriages is common for millions around the world (and growing in the United States as well), the idea of an arranged marriage nevertheless remains outside the mainstream.

The point of this book isn't to convince you to have an arranged marriage or to tell you that they are somehow better. They're not, and I would be the first to admit their flaws. For instance, it's an approach that tends to focus on bringing together people from the same race or religion. And while I can admit that, from what I've seen, it definitely seems to work, it's nonetheless an aspect that sits uncomfortably with my own personal views.

The point of this book has been to show the overarching lesson that love can be learned and that we can control our romantic futures more than we ever realized. Arranged marriages are complex and multilayered institutions that, even with their flaws, demonstrate that creating and obtaining relationship happiness need not be as complex as we make it.

But Are They All Really That Happy?

When I tell people that I spent five years interviewing over three hundred women in arranged marriages, the most common question people ask is, Were they all really that happy?

I've said it earlier, but it's worth repeating. When I say happy, it's not that the women I spoke with were all ecstatic. They weren't. But the overwhelming majority were content and satisfied and, most tellingly, they were not plagued by doubts and questions about their relationships. As we've seen, since these women didn't enter the marriage with unrealistic expectations, they didn't have the sense that they were chasing an impossible ideal. Instead, they were better able to appreciate and enjoy what they did have.

Without a doubt, there had to be an element of self-selection with the women I spoke to. By this, I mean that women who were happy in their arranged marriages were more likely to be willing to be interviewed about their experiences. I did, however, speak with a few women who had had distinctly unhappy arranged marriages and ended up leaving them. Two of them were the result of domestic abuse, and the other adultery. Of course, neither of these two issues are confined to arranged marriages; sadly, they affect women across all cultural and social barriers.

Bringing It All Together

Although each of the lessons in this book can stand alone, they are actually designed to build on each other, fitting in to change the overall way that you approach your dating and relationship life.

One of my main goals was for you realize that we have so much more control over our relationship happiness than we've ever been told or taught. And although it may not be or sound romantic in the way you used to think about these things, it is, when you think about the fact that this means long-term fulfillment is available to all of us. Living happily ever after doesn't depend on the random luck of happening to meet your Mr. Right.

There was so much I learned about relationships, love, and life from the women I interviewed. As I go through my own marriage and adjust to having a child, I find bits of their advice, fragments of the various interviews popping into my mind.

Where to From Here?

Underlying these seven secrets and the arranged-marriage approach are three key themes that should inform and shape your thoughts and relationships going forward.

- Sustained relationship happiness and satisfaction are actually much easier and more attainable then we've been led to believe. If all these women have found long-term relationship contentment, so can you—especially when you remember that it (thankfully!) doesn't actually depend on the blind luck of happening to find the "perfect" partner.

- We've all been seriously brainwashed by a lifetime of exposure to Hollywood and Madison Avenue models of love, romance, and sex, and along the way, we've adopted these as our norms and wants. But not anymore! The definition of romance, love, sexual satisfaction, and daily happiness is entirely up to every woman to define for herself.

- Whom we marry, how it happens, and the patterns we set up in our relationship are all much too important to be left to chance or to passively wait to see what will happen or how.

Ultimately, if you can take one thing away from this book, I would hope it is that with the arranged-marriage approach, you can take charge of your life, relationship, and marriage and set yourself up to be happy. I can think of no better message to share with women in today's complicated world.

Five years ago, I never would have believed that I love being married to my husband as much as I do. This doesn't mean I'm happy every day. I'm not. And it doesn't mean that I don't think about things I would like to change or wonder about roads not taken. I do. But my expectations of marriage have changed and, because of this, I am able to appreciate and savor the many, many great things about my husband and my marriage and let go of the little things that don't matter much anyway. Because I determined my marriage musts and found a man who fulfills them, I am able to look confidently to our future together without any doubts or regrets.

I know that if you give the seven lessons from arranged marriages a chance, the same happy ending awaits you. Good luck!

Author's Note

Do you have a story to share? Visit my website at www.firstcomesmarriage.com and tell me your tale!

About the Author

Reva Seth's expertise on the topic of arranged marriage comes from growing up in a South Asian family full of arranged marriages. Since the age of 8, when she first realized that her parents, unlike those of her friends or the people she saw on TV, had never actually dated, she was fascinated by the subject. Five years ago, Reva began interviewing women in the United States, Canada, and Europe who had chosen to have an arranged marriage. Besides serving as the basis for this book, Reva credits these interviews with helping her to meet her husband of four years as well as deciding to become engaged to him after only the seventh time they met in person. They now have a son, born in 2006.

Born in Toronto, Reva has lived, studied, and worked in a number of different countries, including Bahrain, Canada, India, the United Kingdom, Switzerland, Venezuela, and the United States. Trained as a lawyer, Reva's professional experience includes several years of journalism and public relations, as well as government policy work and corporate law. Reva has published several articles on arranged marriage for British and Canadian national newspapers, such as the *Daily Mail* and the *Globe and Mail*.